Commanders of the French & Indian War

Commanders of the French & Indian War

The Winning of Canada: a Chronicle of
Wolfe

The Passing of New France: a Chronicle of
Montcalm

William Wood

LEONAUR

Commanders of the French & Indian War
The Winning of Canada: a Chronicle of Wolfe
and
The Passing of New France: a Chronicle of Montcalm
by William Wood

First published under the titles
Chronicles of Canada Series: Volume 11 The Winning of Canada: a Chronicle of Wolfe
and
Chronicles of Canada Series: Volume 10 The Passing of New France: a Chronicle of Montcalm

FIRST EDITION

Leonaur is an imprint
of Oakpast Ltd

ISBN: 978-0-85706-862-0 (hardcover)
ISBN: 978-0-85706-863-7 (softcover)

http://www.leonaur.com

Publisher's Notes

The views expressed in this book are not necessarily
those of the publisher.

Contents

JAMES WOLFE

The Winning of Canada: a Chronicle of
Wolfe

Contents

To
My
Mother

Author's Note

Any life of Wolfe can be artificially simplified by treating his purely military work as something complete in itself and not as a part of a greater whole. But, since such treatment gives a totally false idea of his achievement, this little sketch, drawn straight from original sources, tries to show him as he really was, a co-worker with the British fleet in a war based entirely on naval strategy and inseparably connected with international affairs of world-wide significance. The only simplification attempted here is that of arrangement and expression.

W.W.

Quebec, April 1914.

CHAPTER 1

The Boy 1727-1741

Wolfe was a soldier born. Many of his ancestors had stood ready to fight for king and country at a moment's notice. His father fought under the great Duke of Marlborough in the war against France at the beginning of the eighteenth century. His grandfather, his great-grandfather, his only uncle, and his only brother were soldiers too. Nor has the martial spirit deserted the descendants of the Wolfes in the generation now alive. They are soldiers still. The present head of the family, who represented it at the celebration of the tercentenary of the founding of Quebec, fought in Egypt for Queen Victoria; and the member of it who represented Wolfe on that occasion, in the pageant of the Quebec campaign, is an officer in the Canadian army under George V.

The Wolfes are of an old and honourable line. Many hundreds of years ago their forefathers lived in England and later on in Wales. Later still, in the fifteenth century, before America was discovered, they were living in Ireland. Wolfe's father, however, was born in England; and, as there is no evidence that any of his ancestors in Ireland had married other than English Protestants, and as Wolfe's mother was also English, we may say that the victor of Quebec was a pure-bred Englishman. Among his Anglo-Irish kinsmen were the Goldsmiths and the Seymours. Oliver Goldsmith himself was always very proud of being a cousin of the man who took Quebec.

Wolfe's mother, to whom he owed a great deal of his genius; was a descendant of two good families in Yorkshire. She was eighteen years younger than his father, and was very tall and handsome. Wolfe thought there was no one like her. When he was a colonel, and had been through the wars and at court, he still believed she was 'a match for all the beauties.' He was not lucky enough to take after her in looks, except in her one weak feature, a cutaway chin. His body, indeed, seems to have been made up of the bad points of both parents: he had his rheumatism from his father. But his spirit was made up of all their good points; and no braver ever lived in any healthy body than in his own sickly, lanky six foot three.

Wolfe's parents went to live at Westerham in Kent shortly after they were married; and there, on January 2, 1727, in the vicarage—where Mrs Wolfe was staying while her husband was away on duty with his regiment—the victor of Quebec was born. Two other houses in the little country town of Westerham are full of memories of Wolfe. One of these was his father's, a house more than two hundred years old when he was born. It was built in the reign of Henry VII, and the loyal subject who built it had the king's coat of arms carved over the big stone fireplace. Here Wolfe and his younger brother Edward used to sit in the winter evenings with their mother, while their veteran father told them the story of his long campaigns.

So, curiously enough, it appears that Wolfe, the soldier who won Canada for England in 1759, sat under the arms of the king in whose service the sailor Cabot hoisted the flag of England over Canadian soil in 1497. This house has been called Quebec House ever since the victory in 1759. The other house is Squerryes Court, belonging then and now to the Warde family, the Wolfes' closest friends. Wolfe and George Warde were chums from the first day they met. Both wished to go into the army; and both, of course, 'played soldiers,' like other virile boys. Warde lived to be an old man and actually did become a famous cavalry leader. Perhaps when he charged a real enemy, sword in hand, at the head of thundering squadrons, it may have flashed through his mind how he and Wolfe had waved their whips and cheered like mad when they galloped their ponies down the common with nothing but their barking dogs behind them.

Wolfe's parents presently moved to Greenwich, where he was sent to school at Swinden's. Here he worked quietly enough till just before he entered on his 'teens. Then the long-pent rage of England suddenly burst in war with Spain. The people went wild when the British fleet took Porto Bello, a Spanish port in Central America. The news was cried through the streets all night. The noise of battle seemed to be sounding all round Swinden's school, where most of the boys belonged to naval and military families. Ships were fitting out in English harbours. Soldiers were marching into every English camp. Crowds were singing and cheering. First one boy's father and then another's was under orders for the front. Among them was Wolfe's father, who was made adjutant-general to the forces assembling in the Isle of Wight. What were history and geography and mathematics now, when a whole nation was afoot to fight! And who would not fight the Spaniards when they cut off British sailors' ears? That was an old tale by this time; but the flames of anger threw it into lurid relief once more.

Wolfe was determined to go and fight. Nothing could stop him. There was no commission for him as an officer. Never mind! He would go as a volunteer and win his commission in the field. So, one hot day in July 1740, the lanky, red-haired boy of thirteen-and-a-half took his seat on the Portsmouth coach beside his father, the veteran soldier of fifty-five. His mother was a woman of much too fine a spirit to grudge anything for the service of her country; but she could not help being exceptionally anxious about the dangers of disease for a sickly boy in a far-off land of pestilence and fever. She had written to him the very day he left. But he, full of the stir and excitement of a big camp, had carried the letter in his pocket for two or three days before answering it. Then he wrote her the first of many letters from different seats of war, the last one of all being written just before he won the victory that made him famous round the world.

Newport, Isle of Wight, August 6th, 1740.
I received my dearest Mamma's letter on Monday last, but could not answer it then, by reason I was at camp to see the regiments off to go on board, and was too late for the post; but am very sorry, dear Mamma, that you doubt my love, which I'm sure is as sincere as ever any son's was to his mother.
Papa and I are just going on board, but I believe shall not sail this fortnight; in which time, if I can get ashore at Portsmouth or any other town, I will certainly write to you, and, when we are gone, by every ship we meet, because I know it is my duty. Besides, if it is not, I would do it out of love, with pleasure.
I am sorry to hear that your head is so bad, which I fear is caused by your being so melancholy; but pray, dear Mamma, if you love me, don't give yourself up to fears for us. I hope, if it please God, we shall soon see one another, which will be the happiest day that ever I shall see. I will, as sure as I live, if it is possible for me, let you know everything that has happened, by every ship; therefore pray, dearest Mamma, don't doubt about it.

I am in a very good state of health, and am likely to continue so. Pray my love to my brother. Pray my service to Mr Streton and his family, to Mr and Mrs Weston, and to George Warde when you see him; and pray believe me to be, my dearest Mamma, your most dutiful, loving and affectionate son,

J. Wolfe.

To Mrs. Wolfe, at her house in Greenwich, Kent.

Wolfe's 'very good state of health' was not 'likely to continue so,' either in camp or on board ship. A long peace had made the country indifferent to the welfare of the Army and Navy. Now men were suddenly being massed together in camps and fleets as if on Purpose to breed disease. Sanitation on a large scale, never having been practised in peace, could not be improvised in this hurried, though disastrously slow, preparation for a war. The ship in which Wolfe was to sail had been lying idle for years; and her pestilential bilge-water soon began to make the sailors and soldiers sicken and die. Most fortunately, Wolfe was among the first to take ill; and so he was sent home in time to save him from the fevers of Spanish America.

Wolfe was happy to see his mother again, to have his pony to ride and his dogs to play with. But, though he tried his best to stick to his lessons, his heart was wild for the war. He and George Warde used to go every day during the Christmas holidays behind the pigeon-house at Squerryes Court and practise with their swords and pistols. One day they stopped when they heard the post-horn blowing at the gate; and both of them became very much excited when George's father came out himself with a big official envelope marked 'On His Majesty's Service' and addressed to 'James Wolfe, Esquire.' Inside was a commission as second lieutenant in the Marines, signed by George II and dated at St James's Palace, November 3, 1741. Eighteen years later, when the fame of the conquest of Canada was the talk of the kingdom, the Wardes had a stone monument built to mark the spot where Wolfe was standing when the squire handed him his first commission. And there it is today; and on it are the verses ending,

This spot so sacred will forever claim
A proud alliance with its hero's name.

Wolfe was at last an officer. But the Marines were not the corps for him. Their service companies were five thousand miles away, while war with France was breaking out much nearer home. So what was his delight at receiving another commission, on March 25, 1742, as an

18

ensign in the 12th Regiment of Foot! He was now fifteen, an officer, a soldier born and bred, eager to serve his country, and just appointed to a regiment ordered to the front! Within a month an army such as no one had seen since the days of Marlborough had been assembled at Blackheath. Infantry, cavalry, artillery, and engineers, they were all there when King George II, the Prince of Wales, and the Duke of Cumberland came down to review them. Little did anybody think that the tall, eager ensign carrying the colours of the 12th past His Majesty was the man who was to play the foremost part in winning Canada for the British crown.

CHAPTER 2

The Young Soldier 1741-1748

Wolfe's short life may be divided into four periods, all easy to remember, because all are connected with the same number—seven. He was fourteen years a boy at home, with one attempt to be a soldier. This period lasted from 1727 to 1741. Then he was seven years a young officer in time of war, from 1741 to 1748. Then he served seven years more in time of peace, from 1748 to 1755. Lastly, he died in the middle, at the very climax, of the world-famous Seven Years' War, in 1759.

After the royal review at Blackheath in the spring of 1742 the army marched down to Deptford and embarked for Flanders. Wolfe was now off to the very places he had heard his father tell about again and again. The surly Flemings were still the same as when his father knew them. They hated their British allies almost as much as they hated their enemies. The long column of redcoats marched through a scowling mob of citizens, who meanly grudged a night's lodging to the very men coming there to fight for them. We may be sure that Wolfe thought little enough of such mean people as he stepped out with the colours flying above his head. The army halted at Ghent, an ancient city, famous for its trade and wealth, and defended by walls which had once resisted Marlborough.

At first there was a good deal to do and see; and George Warde was there too, as an officer in a cavalry regiment. But Warde had to march away; and Wolfe was left without any companion of his own age, to pass his spare time the best way he could. Like another famous soldier, Frederick the Great,[1] who first won his fame in this very war, he was fond of music and took lessons on the flute. He also did his best to im-

1. *Frederick the Great & the Seven Years' War* by F. W. Longman also published by Leonaur.

prove his French; and when Warde came back the two friends used to go to the French theatre. Wolfe put his French to other use as well, and read all the military books he could find time for. He always kept his kit ready to pack; so that he could have marched anywhere within two hours of receiving the order. And, though only a mere boy-officer, he began to learn the duties of an adjutant, so that he might be fit for promotion whenever the chance should come.

Months wore on and Wolfe was still at Ghent. He had made friends during his stay, and he tells his mother in September: 'This place is full of officers, and we never want company. I go to the play once or twice a week, and talk a little with the ladies, who are very civil and speak French.'

Before Christmas it had been decided at home—where the war-worn father now was, after a horrible campaign at Cartagena—that Edward, the younger son, was also to be allowed to join the army. Wolfe was delighted. 'My brother is much to be commended for the pains he takes to improve himself. I hope to see him soon in Flanders, when, in all probability, before next year is over, we may know something of our trade.' And so they did!

The two brothers marched for the Rhine early in 1743, both in the same regiment. James was now sixteen, Edward fifteen. The march was a terrible one for such delicate boys. The roads were ankle-deep in mud; the weather was vile; both food and water were very bad. Even the dauntless Wolfe had to confess to his mother that he was 'very much fatigued and out of order. I never come into quarters without aching hips and knees.' Edward, still more delicate, was sent off on a foraging party to find something for the regiment to eat. He wrote home to his father from Bonn on April 7:

We can get nothing upon our march but eggs and bacon and sour bread. I have no bedding, nor can get it anywhere. We had a sad march last Monday in the morning. I was obliged to walk up to my knees in snow, though my brother and I have a horse between us. I have often lain upon straw, and should oftener, had I not known some French, which I find very useful; though I was obliged the other day to speak *Latin* for a good dinner. We send for everything we want to the priest.

That summer, when the king arrived with his son the Duke of Cumberland, the British and Hanoverian army was reduced to 37,000 half-fed men. Worse still, the old general, Lord Stair, had led it into a very bad place. These 37,000 men were cooped up on the narrow side of the valley of the river Main, while a much larger French army was on the better side, holding bridges by which to cut them off and attack them while they were all clumped together. Stair tried to slip away in the night. But the French, hearing of this attempt, sent 12,000 men across the river to hold the place the British general was leaving, and 30,000 more, under the Duc de Gramont, to block the road at the place towards which he was evidently marching. At daylight the British and Hanoverians found themselves cut off, both front and rear, while a third French force was waiting to pounce on whichever end showed weakness first. The King of England, who was also Elector of Hanover, would be a great prize, and the French were eager to capture him. This was how the armies faced each other on the morning of June 27, 1743, at Dettingen, the last battlefield on which any king of England has fought in person, and the first for Wolfe.

The two young brothers were now about to see a big battle, like those of which their father used to tell them. Strangely enough, Amherst, the future commander-in-chief in America, under whom Wolfe served at Louisbourg, and the two men who succeeded Wolfe in command at Quebec—Monckton and Townshend—were also there. It is an awful moment for a young soldier, the one before his first great fight. And here were nearly a hundred thousand men, all in full view of each other, and all waiting for the word to begin.

It was a beautiful day, and the sun shone down on a splendidly martial sight. There stood the British and Hanoverians, with wooded hills on their right, the river and the French on their left, the French in their rear, and the French very strongly posted on the rising ground straight in their front. The redcoats were in dense columns, their bayonets flashing and their colours waving defiance. Side by side with their own red cavalry were the black German *cuirassiers*, the blue German lancers, and the gaily dressed green and scarlet Hungarian hussars. The long white lines of the three French armies, varied with royal blue, encircled them on three sides. On the fourth were the leafy green hills.

Wolfe was acting as adjutant and helping the major. His regiment had neither colonel nor lieutenant-colonel with it that day; so he had plenty to do, riding up and down to see that all ranks understood the order that they were not to fire till they were close to the French and were given the word for a volley. He cast a glance at his brother, standing straight and proudly with the regimental colours that he himself had carried past the king at Blackheath the year before. He was not anxious about 'Ned'; he knew how all the Wolfes could fight. He was not anxious about himself; he was only too eager for the fray. A first battle tries every man, and few have not dry lips, tense nerves, and beating hearts at its approach. But the great anxiety of an officer going into action for the first time with untried men is for them and not for himself. The agony of wondering whether they will do well or not is worse, a thousand times, than what he fears for his own safety.

Presently the French gunners, in the centre of their position across the Main, lit their matches and, at a given signal, fired a salvo into the British rear. Most of the baggage wagons were there; and, as the shot and shell began to knock them over, the drivers were seized with a panic. Cutting the traces, these men galloped off up the hills and into the woods as hard as they could go. Now battery after battery began to thunder, and the fire grew hot all round. The king had been in the rear, as he did not wish to change the command on the eve of the battle. But, seeing the panic, he galloped through the whole of his army to show that he was going to fight beside his men. As he passed, and the men saw what he intended to do, they cheered and cheered, and took heart so boldly that it was hard work to keep them from rushing up the heights of Dettingen, where Gramont's 30,000 Frenchmen were waiting to shoot them down.

Across the river Marshal Noailles, the French commander-in-chief, saw the sudden stir in the British ranks, heard the roaring hurrahs, and supposed that his enemies were going to be fairly caught against Gramont in front. In this event he could finish their defeat himself by an overwhelming attack in flank. Both his own and Gramont's artillery now redoubled their fire, till the British could hardly stand it. But then, to the rage and despair of Noailles, Gramont's men, thinking the day was theirs, suddenly left their strong position and charged down on to the same level as the British, who were only too pleased to meet them there. The king, seeing what a happy turn things were taking, galloped along the front of his army, waving his sword and calling out, 'Now, boys! Now for the honour of England!' His horse, maddened by the din, plunged and reared, and would have run away with him, straight in among the French, if a young officer called Trapaud had not seized the reins. The king then dismounted and put himself at the head of his troops, where he remained fighting, sword in hand, till the battle was over.

Wolfe and his major rode along the line of their regiment for the last time. There was not a minute to lose. Down came the Royal Musketeers of France, full gallop, smash. through the Scots Fusiliers and into the line in rear, where most of them were unhorsed and killed. Next, both sides advanced their cavalry, but without advantage to either. Then, with a clear front once more, the main bodies of the French and British infantry rushed together for a fight to a finish. Nearly all of Wolfe's regiment were new to war and too excited to hold their fire. When they were within range, and had halted for a moment to steady the ranks, they brought their muskets down to the 'present.'

The French fell flat on their faces and the bullets whistled harmlessly over them. Then they sprang to their feet and poured in a steady volley while the British were reloading. But the second British volley went home. When the two enemies closed on each other with the bayonet, like the meeting of two stormy seas, the British fought with such fury that the French ranks were broken. Soon the long white waves rolled back and the long red waves rolled forward. Dettingen was reached and the desperate fight was won.

Both the boy-officers wrote home, Edward to his mother, James to his father. Here is a part of Edward's letter:

My brother and self escaped in the engagement and, thank God, are as well as ever we were in our lives, after not only being cannonaded two hours and three-quarters, and fighting with small arms (muskets and bayonets) two hours and one-quarter, but lay the two following nights upon our arms; whilst it rained for about twenty hours in the same time, yet are ready and as capable to do the same again. The Duke of Cumberland behaved charmingly. Our regiment has got a great deal of honour, for we were in the middle of the first line, and in the greatest danger. My brother has wrote to my father and I believe has given him a small account of the battle, so I hope you will excuse it me.

A manly and soldier-like letter for a boy of fifteen! Wolfe's own is much longer and full of touches that show how cool and observant he was, even in his first battle and at the age of only sixteen. Here is some of it:

The *Gens d'Armes*, or *Mousquetaires Gris*, attacked the first line, composed of nine regiments of English foot, and four or five of Austrians, and some Hanoverians. But before they got to the second line, out of two hundred there were not forty living. These unhappy men were of the first families in France.

24

Nothing, I believe, could be more rash than their undertaking. The third and last attack was made by the foot on both sides. We advanced towards one another; our men in high spirits, and very impatient for fighting, being elated with beating the French Horse, part of which advanced towards us; while the rest attacked our Horse, but were soon driven back by the great fire we gave them. The major and I (for we had neither colonel nor lieutenant-colonel), before they came near, were employed in begging and ordering the men not to fire at too great a distance, but to keep it till the enemy should come near us; but to little purpose.

The whole fired when they thought they could reach them, which had like to have ruined us. However, we soon rallied again, and attacked them with great fury, which gained us a complete victory, and forced the enemy to retire in great haste. We got the sad news of the death of as good and brave a man as any amongst us, General Clayton. His death gave us all sorrow, so great was the opinion we had of him. He had, 'tis said, orders for pursuing the enemy, and if we had followed them, they would not have repassed the Main with half their number. Their loss is computed to be between six and seven thousand men, and ours three thousand. His Majesty was in the midst of the fight; and the duke behaved as bravely as a man could do. I had several times the honour of speaking with him just as the battle began and was often afraid of his being dashed to pieces by the cannon-balls. He gave his orders with a great deal of calmness and seemed quite unconcerned. The soldiers were in high delight to have him so near them. I sometimes thought I had lost poor Ned when I saw arms, legs, and heads beat off close by him. A horse I rid of the colonel's, at the first attack, was shot in one of his hinder legs and threw me; so I was obliged to do the duty of an adjutant all that and the next day on foot, in a pair of heavy boots. Three days after the battle I got the horse again, and he is almost well.

Shortly after Dettingen Wolfe was appointed adjutant and promoted to a lieutenancy. In the next year he was made a captain in the 4th Foot while his brother became a lieutenant in the 12th. After this they had very few chances of meeting; and Edward, who had caught a deadly chill, died alone in Flanders, not yet seventeen years old. Wolfe wrote home to his mother:

> Poor Ned wanted nothing but the satisfaction of seeing his
> dearest friends to leave the world with the greatest tranquillity.
> It gives me many uneasy hours when I reflect on the possibility
> there was of my being with him before he died. God knows it
> was not apprehending the danger the poor fellow was in; and
> even that would not have hindered it had I received the physi-
> cian's first letter. I know you won't be able to read this without
> shedding tears, as I do writing it.
>
> Though it is the custom of the army to sell the deceased's ef-
> fects, I could not suffer it. We none of us want, and I thought
> the best way would be to bestow them on the deserving whom
> he had an esteem for in his lifetime. To his servant—the most
> honest and faithful man I ever knew—I gave all his clothes. I
> gave his horse to his friend Parry. I know he loved Parry; and
> for that reason the horse will be taken care of. His other horse
> I keep myself. I have his watch, sash, gorget, books, and maps,
> which I shall preserve to his memory. He was an honest and
> good lad, had lived very well, and always discharged his duty
> with the cheerfulness becoming a good officer. He lived and
> died as a son of you two should. There was no part of his life
> that makes him dearer to me than what you so often men-
> tioned—*he pined after me.*

It was this pining to follow Wolfe to the wars that cost poor Ned
his life. But did not Wolfe himself pine to follow his father?

The next year, 1745, the Young Pretender, 'Bonnie Prince Charlie,'
raised the Highland clans on behalf of his father, won several battles,
and invaded England, in the hope of putting the Hanoverian Georges
off the throne of Great Britain and regaining it for the exiled Stuarts.
The Duke of Cumberland was sent to crush him; and with the duke
went Wolfe. Prince Charlie's army retreated and was at last brought
to bay on Culloden Moor, six miles from Inverness. The Highlanders were not in good spirits after their long retreat before the duke's
army, which enjoyed an immense advantage in having a fleet following it along the coast with plenty of provisions, while the prince's
wretched army was half starved. We may be sure the lesson was not
lost on Wolfe. Nobody understood better than he that the fleet is the
first thing to consider in every British war. And nobody saw a better
example of this than he did afterwards in Canada.

At daybreak on April 16, 1746, the Highlanders found the duke's army marching towards Inverness, and drew up in order to prevent it. Both armies halted, each hoping the other would make the mistake of charging. At last, about one o'clock, the Highlanders in the centre and right could be held back no longer. So eager were they to get at the redcoats that most of them threw down their muskets without even firing them, and then rushed on furiously, sword in hand. "Twas for a time,' said Wolfe, 'a dispute between the swords and bayonets, but the latter was found by far the most destructable (*sic*) weapon.' No quarter was given or taken on either side during an hour of desperate fighting hand to hand. By that time the steady ranks of the redcoats, aided by the cavalry, had killed five times as many as they had lost by the wild slashing of the claymores. The Highlanders turned and fled. The Stuart cause was lost forever.

Again another year of fighting: this time in Holland, where the British, Dutch, and Austrians under the Duke of Cumberland met the French at the village of Laffeldt, on June 21, 1747. Wolfe was now a brigade-major, which gave him the same sort of position in a brigade of three battalions as an adjutant has in a single one; that is, he was a smart junior officer picked out to help the brigadier in command by seeing that orders were obeyed. The fight was furious. As fast as the British infantry drove back one French brigade another came forward and drove the British back. The village was taken and lost, lost and taken, over and over again. Wolfe, though wounded, kept up the fight.

At last a new French brigade charged in and swept the British out altogether. Then the duke ordered the Dutch and Austrians to advance: But the Dutch cavalry, right in the centre, were seized with a sudden panic and galloped back, knocking over their own men on the way, and making a gap that certainly looked fatal. But the right man was ready to fill it. This was Sir John Ligonier, afterwards commander-in-chief of the British Army at the time of Wolfe's campaigns in Canada. He led the few British and Austrian cavalry, among them the famous Scots Greys, straight into the gap and on against the dense masses of the French beyond. These gallant horsemen were doomed; and of course they knew it when they dashed themselves to death against such overwhelming odds. But they gained the few precious moments that were needed. The gap closed up behind them; and the army was saved, though they were lost.

During the day Wolfe was several times in great danger. He was thanked by the duke in person for the splendid way in which he had done his duty. The royal favour, however, did not make him forget the gallant conduct of his faithful servant, Roland:

> He came to me at the hazard of his life with offers of his service, took off my cloak and brought a fresh horse; and would have continued close by me had I not ordered him to retire. I believe he was slightly wounded just at that time. Many a time has he pitched my tent and made the bed ready to receive me, half-dead with fatigue.

Nor did Wolfe forget his dumb friends:

> I have sold my poor little gray mare. I lamed her by accident, and thought it better to dismiss her the service immediately. I grieved at parting with so faithful a servant, and have the comfort to know she is in good hands, will be very well fed, and taken care of in her latter days.

After recovering from a slight wound received at Laffeldt Wolfe was allowed to return to England, where he remained for the winter. On the morrow of New Year's Day, 1748, he celebrated his coming of age at his father's town house in Old Burlington Street, London. In the spring, however, he was ordered to rejoin the army, and was stationed with the troops who were guarding the Dutch frontier. The war came to an end in the same year, and Wolfe went home. Though then only twenty-one, he was already an experienced soldier, a rising officer, and a marked man.

CHAPTER 3

The Seven Years' Peace 1748-1755

Wolfe was made welcome in England wherever he went. In spite of his youth his name was well known to the chief men in the army, and he was already a hero among the friends of his family. By nature he was fond of the society of ladies, and of course he fell in love. He had had a few flirtations before, like most other soldiers; but this time the case was serious. The difference was the same as between a sham fight and a battle. His choice fell on Elizabeth Lawson, a maid of honour to the Princess of Wales. The oftener he saw her the more he fell in love with her. But the course of true love did not, as we shall presently see, run any more smoothly for him than it has for many another famous man.

In 1749, when Wolfe was only twenty-two, he was promoted major of the 20th Regiment of Foot. He joined it in Scotland, where he was to serve for the next few years. At first he was not very happy in Glasgow. He did not like the people, as they were very different from the friends with whom he had grown up. Yet his loneliness only added to his zeal for study. He had left school when still very young, and he now found himself ignorant of much that he wished to know. As a man of the world he had found plenty of gaps in his general knowledge. Writing to his friend Captain Rickson, he says:

> When a man leaves his studies at fifteen, he will never be justly called a man of letters. I am endeavouring to repair the damages of my education, and have a person to teach me Latin and mathematics.

From his experience in his own profession, also, he had learned a good deal. In a letter to his father he points out what excellent chances soldiers have to see the vivid side of many things:

That variety incident to a military life gives our profession some advantages over those of a more even nature. We have all our passions and affections aroused and exercised, many of which must have wanted their proper employment had not suitable occasions obliged us to exert them. Few men know their own courage till danger proves them, or how far the love of honour or dread of shame are superior to the love of life. This is a knowledge to be best acquired in an army; our actions are there in presence of the world, to be fully censured or approved.

Great commanders are always keen to learn everything really worthwhile. It is only the little men who find it a bore. Of course, there are plenty of little men in a regiment, as there are everywhere else in the world; and some of the officers were afraid Wolfe would insist on their doing as he did. But he never preached. He only set the example, and those who had the sense could follow it. One of his captains wrote home:

Our acting colonel here is a paragon. He neither drinks, curses, nor gambles. So we make him our pattern.

After a year with him the officers found him a 'jolly good fellow' as well as a pattern; and when he became their lieutenant-colonel at twenty-three they gave him a dinner that showed he was a prime favourite among them. He was certainly quite as popular with the men. Indeed, he soon became known by a name which speaks for itself— 'the soldier's' friend.'

By and by Wolfe's regiment marched into the Highlands, where he had fought against Prince Charlie in the '45. But he kept in touch with what was going on in the world outside. He wrote to Rickson at Halifax, to find out for him all he could about the French and British colonies in America. In the same letter, written in 1751, he said he should like to see some Highland soldiers raised for the king's army and sent out there to fight. Eight years later he was to have a Highland regiment among his own army at Quebec. Other themes filled the letters to his mother. Perhaps he was thinking of Miss Lawson when he wrote:

I have a certain turn of mind that favours matrimony prodigiously. I love children. Two or three manly sons are a present to the world, and the father that offers them sees with satisfaction that he is to live in his successors.

He was thinking more gravely of a still higher thing when he wrote on his twenty-fifth birthday, January 2, 1752, to reassure his mother about the strength of his religion.

Later on in the year, having secured leave of absence, he wrote to his mother in the best of spirits. He asked her to look after all the little things he wished to have done.

> Mr Pattison sends a pointer to Blackheath; if you will order him to be tied up in your stable, it will oblige me much. If you hear of a servant who can dress a wig it will be a favour done me to engage him. I have another favour to beg of you and you'll think it an odd one: 'tis to order some currant jelly to be made in a crock for my use. It is the custom in Scotland to eat it in the morning with bread.

Then he proposed to have a shooting-lodge in the Highlands, long before any other Englishman seems to have thought of what is now so common.

> You know what a whimsical sort of person I am. Nothing pleases me now but hunting, shooting, and fishing. I have distant notions of taking a very little house, remote upon the edge of the forest, merely for sport.

In July he left the Highlands, which were then, in some ways, as wild as Labrador is now. About this time there was a map made by a Frenchman in Paris which gave all the chief places in the Lowlands quite rightly, but left the north of Scotland blank, with the words 'Unknown land here, inhabited by the "*Iglandaires*"!' When his leave began Wolfe went first to Dublin—'dear, dirty Dublin,' as it used to be called—where his uncle, Major Walter Wolfe, was living. He wrote to his father:

> The streets are crowded with people of a large size and well limbed, and the women very handsome. They have clearer skins, and fairer complexions than the women in England or Scotland, and are exceeding straight and well made.

—which shows that he had the proper soldier's eye for every pretty girl. Then he went to London and visited his parents in their new house at the corner of Greenwich Park, which stands today very much the same as it was then. But, wishing to travel, he succeeded, after a great deal of trouble, in getting leave to go to Paris. Lord Bury was a friend of his, and Lord Bury's father, the Earl of Albemarle, was the British ambassador there. So he had a good chance of seeing the best of everything. Perhaps it would be almost as true to say that he had as good a chance of seeing the worst of everything. For there were a great many corrupt and corrupting men and women at the French court. There was also much misery in France, and both the corruption and the misery were soon to trouble New France, as Canada was then called, even more than they troubled Old France at home.

Wolfe wished to travel about freely, to see the French armies at work, and then to go on to Prussia to see how Frederick the Great managed his perfectly disciplined army. This would have been an excellent thing to do. But it was then a very new thing for an officer to ask leave to study foreign armies. Moreover, the chief men in the British Army did not like the idea of letting such a good colonel go away from his regiment for a year, even though he was going with the object of making himself a still better officer. Perhaps, too, his friends were just a little afraid that he might join the Prussians or the Austrians; for it was not, in those days, a very strange thing to join the army of a friendly foreign country. Whatever the reason, the long leave was refused and he went no farther than Paris.

Louis XV was then at the height of his apparent greatness; and France was a great country, as it is still. But king and government were both corrupt. Wolfe saw this well enough and remembered it when the next war broke out. There was a brilliant society in 'the capital of civilization,' as the people of Paris proudly called their city; and there was a great deal to see. Nor was all of it bad. He wrote home two days after his arrival.

The packet [ferry] did not sail that night, but we embarked at half-an-hour after six in the morning and got into Calais at ten. I never suffered so much in so short a time at sea. The people (in Paris) seem to be very sprightly. The buildings are very magnificent, far surpassing any we have in London. Mr Selwin has recommended a French master to me, and in a few days I begin to ride in the Academy, but must dance and fence in my own lodgings. Lord Albemarle (the British ambassador) is come from Fontainebleau. I have very good reason to be pleased with the reception I met with. The best amusement for strangers in Paris is the Opera, and the next is the playhouse. The theatre is a school to acquire the French language, for which reason I frequent it more than the other.

In Paris he met young Philip Stanhope, the boy to whom the Earl of Chesterfield wrote his celebrated letters; 'but,' says Wolfe, 'I fancy he is infinitely inferior to his father.' Keeping fit, as we call it nowadays, seems to have been Wolfe's first object. He took the same care of himself as the Japanese officers did in the Russo-Japanese War; and for the same reason, that he might be the better able to serve his country well the next time she needed him. Writing to his mother he says:

I am up every morning at or before seven and fully employed till twelve. Then I dress and visit, and dine at two. At five most people go to the public entertainments, which keep you till nine; and at eleven I am always in bed. This way of living is directly opposite to the practice of the place. But no constitution could go through all. Four or five days in the week I am up six hours before any other fine gentleman in Paris. I ride, fence, dance, and have a master to teach me French. I succeed much better in fencing and riding than in the art of dancing, for they suit my genius better; and I improve a little in French. I have no great acquaintance with the French women, nor am likely to have. It is almost impossible to introduce one's self among them without losing a great deal of money, which you know I can't afford; besides, these entertainments begin at the time I go to bed, and I have not health enough to sit up all night and work all day. The people here use umbrellas to defend them from the sun, and something of the same kind to secure them from the rain and snow. I wonder a practice so useful is not introduced into England.

While in Paris Wolfe was asked if he would care to be military tutor to the Duke of Richmond, or, if not, whether he knew of any good officer whom he could recommend. On this he named Guy Carleton, who became the young duke's tutor. Three men afterwards well known in Canada were thus brought together long before any of them became celebrated. The Duke of Richmond went into Wolfe's regiment. The next duke became a governor-general of Canada, as Guy Carleton had been before him. And Wolfe—well, he was Wolfe!

One day he was presented to King Louis, from whom, seven years later, he was to wrest Quebec. 'They were all very gracious as far as courtesies, bows, and smiles go, for the Bourbons seldom speak to anybody.' Then he was presented to the clever Marquise de Pompadour, whom he found having her hair done up in the way which is still known by her name to every woman in the world. It was the regular custom of that time for great ladies to receive their friends while the barbers were at work on their hair. 'She is extremely handsome and, by her conversation with the ambassador, I judge she must have a great deal of wit and understanding.' But it was her court intrigues and her shameless waste of money that helped to ruin France and Canada.

In the midst of all these gaieties Wolfe never forgot the mother whom he thought 'a match for all the beauties.' He sent her 'two black laced hoods and a *vestale* for the neck, such as the Queen of France wears.' Nor did he forget the much humbler people who looked upon him as 'the soldier's friend.' He tells his mother that his letters from Scotland have just arrived, and that 'the women of the regiment take it into their heads to write to me sometimes.' Here is one of their letters, marked on the outside, 'The Petition of Anne White':

> Collonnell,—Being a true noble-hearted pittyful gentleman and officer your Worship will excuse these few lines concerning ye husband of ye undersigned, Sergt. White, who not from his own fault is not behaving as hee should towards me and his family, although good and faithfull till the middle of November last.

We may be sure 'Sergt. White' had to behave 'as hee should' when Wolfe returned!

In April, to his intense disgust, Wolfe was again in Glasgow.

> We are all sick, officers and soldiers. In two days we lost the skin off our faces with the sun, and the third were shivering in great coats. My cousin Goldsmith has sent me the finest young pointer that ever was seen; he eclipses Workie, and outdoes all. He sent me a fishing-rod and wheel at the same time, of his own workmanship. This, with a salmon-rod from my uncle Wat, your flies, and my own guns, put me in a condition to undertake the Highland sport. We have plays, we have concerts, we have balls, with dinners and suppers of the most execrable food upon earth, and wine that approaches to poison. The men of Glasgow drink till they are excessively drunk. The ladies are cold to everything but a bagpipe—I wrong them—there is not one that does not melt away at the sound of money.

By the end of this year, however, he had left Scotland for good. He did not like the country as he saw it. But the times were greatly against his doing so. Glasgow was not at all a pleasant place in those narrowly provincial days for anyone who had seen much of the world. The Highlands were as bad. They were full of angry Jacobites, who could never forgive the redcoats for defeating Prince Charlie. Yet Wolfe was not against the Scots as a whole; and we must never forget that he was the first to recommend the raising of those Highland regiments which have fought so nobly in every British war since the mighty one in which he fell.

During the next year and part of the year following, 1754-55, Wolfe was at Exeter, where the entertainments seem to have been more to his taste than those at Glasgow. A lady who knew him well at this time wrote:

> He was generally ambitious to gain a tall, graceful woman to be his partner, as well as a good dancer. He seemed emulous to display every kind of virtue and gallantry that would render him amiable.

In 1755 the Seven Years' Peace was coming to an end in Europe. The shadow of the Seven Years' War was already falling darkly across the prospect in America. Though Wolfe did not leave for the front till 1757, he was constantly receiving orders to be ready, first for one place and then for another. So early as February 18, 1755, he wrote to his mother what he then thought might be a farewell letter. It is full of the great war; but personal affairs of the deeper kind were by no means forgotten.

> The success of our fleet in the beginning of the war is of the utmost importance.
> It will be sufficient comfort to you both to reflect that the Power which has hitherto preserved me may, if it be His pleasure, continue to do so. If not, it is but a few days more or less, and those who perish in their duty and the service of their country die honourably.

The end of this letter is in a lighter vein. But it is no less characteristic: it is all about his dogs.

> You are to have Flurry instead of Romp. The two puppies I must desire you to keep a little longer. I can't part with either of them, but must find good and secure quarters for them as well as for my friend Caesar, who has great merit and much good humour. I have given Sancho to Lord Howe, so that I am reduced to two spaniels and one pointer.

It is strange that in the many books about dogs which mention the great men who have been fond of them—and most great men are fond of dogs—not one says a word about Wolfe. Yet 'my friend Caesar, who has great merit and much good humour,' deserves to be remembered with his kind master just as much, in his way, as that other Caesar, the friend of Edward VII, who followed his master to the grave among the kings and princes of a mourning world.

CHAPTER 4

The Seven Years' War 1756-1763

Wolfe's Quebec campaign marked the supreme crisis of the greatest war the British Empire ever waged: the war, indeed, that made the Empire. To get a good, clear view of anything so vast, so complex, and so glorious, we must first look at the whole course of British history to see how it was that France and England ever became such deadly rivals. It is quite wrong to suppose that the French and British were always enemies, though they have often been called 'historic' and 'hereditary' foes, as if they never could make friends at all. As a matter of fact, they have had many more centuries of peace than of war; and ever since the Battle of Waterloo, in 1815, they have been growing friendlier year by year. But this happy state of affairs is chiefly because, as we now say, their 'vital interests no longer clash'; that is, they do not both desire the same thing so keenly that they have to fight for it.

Their vital interests do not clash now. But they did clash twice in the course of their history. The first time was when both governments wished to rule the same parts of the land of France. The second time was when they both wished to rule the same parts of the oversea world. Each time there was a long series of wars, which went on inevitably until one side had completely driven its rival from the field.

The first long series of wars took place chiefly in the fourteenth century and is known to history as the Hundred Years' War. England held, and was determined to hold, certain parts of France. France was determined never to rest till she had won them for herself. Whatever other things the two nations were supposed to be fighting about, this was always the one cause of strife that never changed and never could change till one side or other had definitely triumphed. France won. There were glorious English victories at Cressy and Agincourt.

Edward III and Henry V were two of the greatest soldiers of any age. But, though the English often won the battles, the French won the war. The French had many more men, they fought near their own homes, and, most important of all, the war was waged chiefly on land. The English had fewer men, they fought far away from their homes, and their ships could not help them much in the middle of the land, except by bringing over soldiers and food to the nearest coast. The end of it all was that the English armies were worn out; and the French armies, always able to raise more and more fresh men, drove them, step by step, out of the land completely.

The second long series of wars took place chiefly in the eighteenth century. These wars have never been given one general name; but they should be called the Second Hundred Years' War, because that is what they really were. They were very different from the wars that made up the first Hundred Years' War, because this time the fight was for oversea dominions, not for land in Europe. Of course navies had a good deal to do with the first Hundred Years' War and armies with the second. But the navies were even more important in the second than the armies in the first. The Second Hundred Years' War, the one in which Wolfe did such a mighty deed, began with the fall of the Stuart kings of England in 1688 and went on till the battle of Waterloo in 1815. But the beginning and end that meant most to the Empire were the naval battles of La Hogue in 1692 and Trafalgar in 1805. Since Trafalgar the Empire has been able to keep what it had won before, and to go on growing as well, because all its different parts are joined together by the sea, and because the British Navy has been, from that day to this, stronger than any other navy in the world.

How the French and British armies and navies fought on opposite sides, either alone or with allies, all over the world, from time to time, for these hundred and twenty-seven years; how all the eight wars with different names formed one long Second Hundred Years' War; and how the British Navy was the principal force that won the whole of this war, made the Empire, and gave Canada safety then, as it gives her safety now—all this is much too long a story to tell here. But the gist of it may be told in a very few words, at least in so far as it concerns the winning of Canada and the deeds of Wolfe.

The name 'Greater Britain' is often used to describe all the parts of the British Empire which lie outside of the old mother country. This 'Greater Britain' is now so vast and well established that we are apt to forget those other empires beyond the seas which, each in its own day, surpassed the British Empire of the same period. There was a Greater

Portugal, a Greater Spain, a Greater Holland, and a Greater France. France and Holland still have large oversea possessions; and a whole new-world continent still speaks the languages of Spain and Portugal. But none of them has kept a growing empire oversea as their British rival has. What made the difference? The two things that made all the difference in the world were freedom and sea-power. We cannot stop to discuss freedom, because that is more the affair of statesmen; but, at the same time, we must not forget that the side on which Wolfe fought was the side of freedom. The point for us to notice here is that all the freedom and all the statesmen and all the soldiers put together could never have made a Greater Britain, especially against all those other rivals, unless Wolfe's side had also been the side of sea-power.

Now, sea-power means more than fighting power at sea; it means trading power as well. But a nation cannot trade across the sea against its rivals if its own ships are captured and theirs are not. And long before the Second Hundred Years' War with France the other sea-trading empires had been gradually giving way, because in time of war their ships were always in greater danger than those of the British were. After the English Navy had defeated the Spanish Armada in 1588 the Spaniards began, slowly but surely, to lose their chance of making a permanent Greater Spain. After the great Dutch War, when Blake defeated Van Tromp in 1653, there was no further chance of a permanent Greater Holland. And, even before the Dutch War and the Armada, the Portuguese, who had once ruled the Indian Ocean and who had conquered Brazil, were themselves conquered by Spain and shut out from all chance of establishing a Greater Portugal.

So the one supreme point to be decided by the Second Hundred Years' War lay between only two rivals, France and Britain. Was there to be a Greater France or a Greater Britain across the seas? The answer depended on the rival navies. Of course, it involved many other elements of national and Imperial power on both sides. But no other elements of power could have possibly prevailed against a hostile and triumphant navy.

Everything that went to make a Greater France or a Greater Britain had to cross the sea—men, women, and children, horses and cattle, all the various appliances a civilized people must take with them when they settle in a new country. Every time there was war there were battles at sea, and these battles were nearly always won by the British. Every British victory at sea made it harder for French trade, because every ship between France and Greater France ran more risk o being taken, while every ship between Britain and Greater Britain stood a better chance of getting safely through. This affected everything on both competing sides in America. British business went on. French business almost stopped dead.

Even the trade with the Indians living a thousand miles inland was changed in favour of the British and against the French, as all the guns and knives and beads and everything else that the white man offered to the Indian in exchange for his furs had to come across the sea, which was just like an enemy's country to every French ship, but just like her own to every British one. Thus the victors at sea grew continually stronger in America, while the losers grew correspondingly weaker. When peace came, the French only had time enough to build new ships and start their trade again before the next war set them back once more; while the British had nearly all their old ships, all those they had taken from the French, and many new ones.

But where did Wolfe come in? He came in at the most important time and place of all, and he did the most important single deed of all. This brings us to the consideration of how the whole of the Second Hundred Years' War was won, not by the British Navy alone, much less by the Army alone, but by the united service of both, fighting like the two arms of one body, the Navy being the right arm and the army the left. The heart of this whole Second Hundred Years' War was the Seven Years' War; the British part of the Seven Years' War was then called the 'Maritime War'; and the heart of the 'Maritime War' was the winning of Canada, in which the decisive blow was dealt by Wolfe.

We shall see presently how navy and army worked together as a united service in 'joint expeditions' by sea and land, how Wolfe took part in two other joint expeditions before he commanded the land force of the one at Quebec, and how the mighty empire-making statesman, William Pitt, won the day for Britain and for Greater Britain, with Lord Anson at the head of the navy to help him, and Saunders in command at the front. It was thus that the age-long vexed question of a Greater France or a Greater Britain in America was finally decided by the sword. The conquering sword was that of the British Empire as a whole. But the hand that wielded it was Pitt; the hilt was Anson, the blade was Saunders, and the point was Wolfe.

CHAPTER 5

Louisbourg 1758

In 1755 Wolfe was already writing what he thought were farewell letters before going off to the war. And that very year the war, though not formally declared till the next, actually did break out in America, where a British army under Braddock, with Washington as his *aide-de-camp*, was beaten in Ohio by the French and Indians. Next year the French, owing to the failure of Admiral Byng and the British fleet to assist the garrison, were able to capture Minorca in the Mediterranean; while their new general in Canada, Montcalm, Wolfe's great opponent, took Oswego. The triumph of the French fleet at Minorca made the British people furious. Byng was court-martialled, found guilty of failure to do his utmost to save Minorca, and condemned to death. In spite of Pitt's efforts to save him, the sentence was carried out and he was shot on the quarter-deck of his own flagship. Two other admirals, Hawke and Saunders, both of whom were soon to see service with Wolfe, were then sent out as a 'cargo of courage' to retrieve the British position at sea. By this time preparations were being hurried forward on every hand. Fleets were fitting out. Armies were mustering. And, best of all, Pitt was just beginning to make his influence felt.

In 1757, the third year of war, things still went badly for the British at the front. In America Montcalm took Fort William Henry, and a British fleet and army failed to accomplish anything against Louisbourg. In Europe another British fleet and army were fitted out to go on another joint expedition, this time against Rochefort, a great seaport in the west of France. The senior staff officer, next to the three generals in command, was Wolfe, now thirty years of age. The admiral in charge of the fleet was Hawke, as famous a fighter as Wolfe himself. A little later, when both these great men were known throughout the whole United Service, as well as among the millions in Britain and

WILLIAM PITT, EARL OF CHATHAM

in Greater Britain, their names were coupled in countless punning toasts, and patriots from Canada to Calcutta would stand up to drink a health to 'the eye of a Hawke and the heart of a Wolfe.' But Wolfe was not a general yet; and the three pottering old men who were generals at Rochefort could not make up their minds to do anything but talk. These generals had been ordered to take Rochefort by complete surprise. But after spending five days in front of it, so that every Frenchman could see what they had come for, they decided to countermand the attack and sail home.

Wolfe was a very angry and disgusted man. Yet, though this joint expedition was a disgraceful failure, he had learned some useful lessons, which he was presently to turn to good account. He saw, at least, what such expeditions should not attempt; and that a general should act boldly, though wisely, with the fleet. More than this, he had himself made a plan which his generals were too timid to carry out; and this plan was so good that Pitt, now in supreme control for the next four years, made a note of it and marked him down for promotion and command.

Both came sooner than anyone could have expected. Pitt was sick of fleets and armies that did nothing but hold councils of war and then come back to say that the enemy could not be safely attacked. He made up his mind to send out real fighters with the next joint expedition. So in 1758 he appointed Wolfe as the junior of the three brigadier-generals under Amherst, who was to join Admiral Boscawen—nicknamed 'Old Dreadnought'—in a great expedition meant to take Louisbourg for good and all.

Louisbourg was the greatest fortress in America. It was in the extreme east of Canada, on the island of Cape Breton, near the best fishing-grounds, and on the flank of the ship channel into the St Lawrence. A fortress there, in which French fleets could shelter safely, was like a shield for New France and a sword against New England. In 1745, just before the outbreak of the Jacobite rebellion in Scotland, an army of New Englanders under Sir William Pepperrell, with the assistance of Commodore Warren's fleet, had taken this fortress. But at the peace of Aix-la-Chapelle in 1748, when Wolfe had just come of age, it was given back to France.

Ten years later, when Wolfe went out to join the second army that was sent against it, the situation was extremely critical. Both French and British strained every nerve, the one to hold, the other to take, the greatest fortress in America. A French fleet sailed from Brest in the spring and arrived safely. But it was not nearly strong enough to attempt a sea-fight off Louisbourg, and three smaller fleets that were meant to join it were all smashed up off the coast of France by the British, who thus knew, before beginning the siege, that Louisbourg could hardly expect any help from outside. Hawke was one of the British smashers this year. The next year he smashed up a much greater force in Quiberon Bay, and so made 'the eye of a Hawke and the heart of a Wolfe' work together again, though they were thousands of miles apart and one directed a fleet while the other inspired an army.

The fortress of Louisbourg was built beside a fine harbour with an entrance still further defended by a fortified island. It was garrisoned by about four thousand four hundred soldiers. Some of these were hired Germans, who cared nothing for the French; and the French-Canadian and Indian irregulars were not of much use at a regular siege. The British admiral Boscawen had a large fleet, and General Amherst an army twelve thousand strong. Taking everything into account, by land and sea, the British united service at the siege was quite three times as strong as the French united service. But the French ships, manned by three thousand sailors, were in a good harbour, and they and the soldiers were defended by thick walls with many guns. Besides, the whole defence was conducted by Drucour, as gallant a leader as ever drew sword.

Boscawen was chosen by Pitt for the same reason as Wolfe had been, because he was a fighter. He earned his nickname of 'Old Dreadnought' from the answer he made one night in the English Channel when the officer of the watch called him to say that two big French ships were bearing down on his single British one. 'What are we to do, sir?' asked the officer. 'Do?' shouted Boscawen, springing out of his berth, 'Do?—Why, damn 'em, fight 'em, of course!' And they did. Amherst was the slow-and-sure kind of general; but he had the sense to know a good man when he saw one, and to give Wolfe the chance of trying his own quick-and-sure way instead.

A portion of the British fleet under Vice-Admiral Sir Charles Hardy had been cruising off Louisbourg for some time before Boscawen's squadron hove in sight on June 2. This squadron was followed by more than twice its own number of ships carrying the army. All together, there were a hundred and fifty-seven British vessels, besides Hardy's covering squadron. Of course, the men could not be landed under the fire of the fortress. But two miles south of it, and running westward from it for many miles more, was Gabarus Bay with an open beach.

For several days the Atlantic waves dashed against the shore so furiously that no boat could live through their breakers. But on the eighth the three brigades of infantry made for three different points,[1] respectively two, three, and four miles from the fortress. The French sent out half the garrison to shoot down the first boatloads that came in on the rollers. To cover the landing, some of Boscawen's ships moved in as close as they could and threw shells inshore: but without dislodging the enemy.

Each of the three brigades had its own flag—one red, another blue, and the third white. Wolfe's brigade was the red, the one farthest west from Louisbourg, and Wolfe's did the fighting. While the boats rose and fell on the gigantic rollers and the enemy's cannon roared and the waves broke in thunder on the beach, Wolfe was standing up in the stern-sheets, scanning every inch of the ground to see if there was no place where a few men could get a footing and keep it till the rest had landed. He had first-rate soldiers with him: grenadiers, Highlanders, and light infantry.

The boats were now close in, and the French were firing cannon and muskets into them right and left. One cannon-ball whizzed across Wolfe's own boat and smashed his flagstaff to splinters. Just then three young light infantry officers saw a high ledge of rocks, under shelter of which a few men could form up. Wolfe, directing every movement with his cane, like Gordon in China a century later, shouted to the others to follow them; and then, amid the crash of artillery and the wild welter of the surf, though many boats were smashed and others upset, though some men were shot and others drowned, the landing was securely made. 'Who were the first ashore?' asked Wolfe, as the men were forming up under the ledge. Two Highlanders were pointed out. 'Good fellows!' he said, as he went up to them and handed each a guinea.

While the ranks were forming on the beach, the French were firing into them and men were dropping fast. But every gap was closed as soon as it was made. Directly Wolfe saw he had enough men he sprang to the front; whereupon they all charged after him, straight at the batteries on the crest of the rising shore. Here there was some wild work for a minute or two, with swords, bayonets, and muskets all hard at it. But the French now saw, to their dismay, that thousands of other redcoats were clambering ashore, nearer in to Louisbourg,

---

1. White Point, Flat Point, and Kennington Cove. See the accompanying Map of the siege.

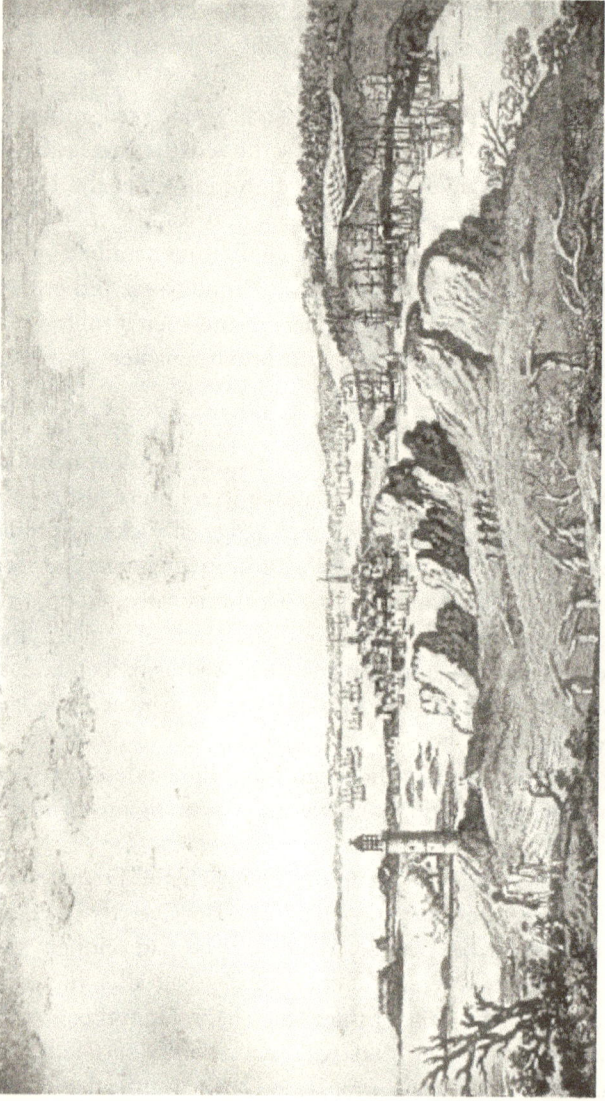

AN ENGRAVED VIEW OF LOUISBOURG IN 1758

and that these men would cut them off if they waited a moment longer. So they turned and ran, hotly pursued, till they were safe in under the guns of the fortress. A deluge of shot and shell immediately belched forth against the pursuing British, who wisely halted just out of range.

After this exciting commencement Amherst's guns, shot, shell, powder, stores, food, tents, and a thousand other things had all to be landed on the surf-lashed, open beach. It was the sailors' stupendous task to haul the whole of this cumbrous material up to the camp. The bluejackets, however, were not the only ones to take part in the work, for the ships' women also turned to, with the best of a gallant goodwill. In a few days all the material was landed; and Amherst, having formed his camp, sat down to conduct the siege.

Louisbourg harbour faces east, runs in westward nearly a mile, and is over two miles from north to south. The north and south points, however, on either side of its entrance, are only a mile apart. On the south point stood the fortress; on the north the lighthouse; and between were several islands, rocks, and bars that narrowed the entrance for ships to only three cables, or a little more than six hundred yards. Wolfe saw that the north point, where the lighthouse stood, was undefended, and might be seized and used as a British battery to smash up the French batteries on Goat Island at the harbour mouth. Acting on this idea, he marched with twelve hundred men across the stretch of country between the British camp and the lighthouse. The fleet brought round his guns and stores and all other necessaries by sea. A tremendous bombardment then silenced every French gun on Goat Island. This left the French nothing for their defence but the walls of Louisbourg itself.

Both French and British soon realized that the fall of Louisbourg was only a question of time. But time was everything to both. The British were anxious to take Louisbourg and then sail up to Quebec and take it by a sudden attack while Montcalm was engaged in fighting Abercromby's army on Lake Champlain. The French, of course, were anxious to hold out long enough to prevent this; and Drucour, their commandant at Louisbourg, was just the man for their purpose. His wife, too, was as brave as he. She used to go round the batteries cheering up the gunners, and paying no more attention to the British shot and shell than if they had been only fireworks. On June 18, just before Wolfe's lighthouse batteries were ready to open fire, Madame Drucour set sail in the venturesome *Echo*, a little French man-of-war that was making a dash for it, in the hope of carrying the news to Quebec. But after a gallant fight the *Echo* had to haul down her colours to the *Juno* and the *Sutherland*. We shall hear more of the *Sutherland* at the supreme moment of Wolfe's career.

Nothing French, not even a single man, could now get into or out of Louisbourg. But Drucour still kept the flag up, and sent out parties at night to harass his assailants. One of these surprised a British post, killed Lord Dundonald who commanded it, and retired safely after being almost cut off by British reinforcements. Though Wolfe had silenced the island batteries and left the entrance open enough for Boscawen to sail in, the admiral hesitated because he thought he might lose too many ships by risking it. Then the French promptly sank some of their own ships at the entrance to keep him out. But six hundred British sailors rowed in at night and boarded and took the only two ships remaining afloat. The others had been blown up a month before by British shells fired by naval gunners from Amherst's batteries.

Drucour was now in a terrible, plight. Not a ship was left. He was completely cut off by land and sea. Many of his garrison were dead, many more were lying sick or wounded. His foreigners were ready for desertion. His French Canadians had grown down-hearted. All the non-combatants wished him to surrender at once. What else could he do but give in? On July 27 he hauled down the *fleurs-de-lis* from the great fortress. But he had gained his secondary object; for it was now much too late in the year for the same British force to begin a new campaign against Quebec.

Wolfe, like Nelson and Napoleon, was never content to 'let well enough alone,' if anything better could possibly be done. When the news came of Montcalm's great victory over Abercromby at Ticonderoga[2], he told Amherst he was ready to march inland at once with reinforcements. And after Louisbourg had surrendered and Boscawen had said it was too late to start for Quebec, he again volunteered to do any further service that Amherst required. The service he was sent on was the soldier's most disgusting duty; but he did it thoroughly, though he would have preferred anything else. He went with Hardy's squadron to destroy the French settlements along the Gulf of St Lawrence, so as to cut off their supplies from the French in Quebec before the next campaign.

2. Montcalm at the Battle of Carillon (Ticonderoga) (July 8th, 1758) by Maurice Sautai also published by Leonaur.

After Rochefort Wolfe had become a marked man. After Louis-bourg he became an Imperial hero. The only other the army had yet produced in this war was Lord Howe, who had been killed in a skirmish just before Ticonderoga. Wolfe knew Howe well, admired him exceedingly, and called him 'the noblest Englishman that has appeared in my time, and the best soldier in the army.' He would have served under him gladly. But Howe—young, ardent, gallant, yet profound—was dead; and the hopes of discerning judges were centred on Wolfe. The war had not been going well, and this victory at Louisbourg was the first that the British people could really rejoice over with all their heart.

The British colonies went wild with delight. Halifax had a state ball, at which Wolfe danced to his heart's content; while his unofficial partners thought themselves the luckiest girls in all America to be asked by the hero of Louisbourg. Boston and Philadelphia had large bonfires and many fireworks. The chief people of New York attended a gala dinner. Every church had special thanksgivings.

In England the excitement was just as great, and Wolfe's name and fame flew from lip to lip all over the country. Parliament passed special votes of thanks. Medals were struck to celebrate the event. The king stood on his palace steps to receive the captured colours, which were carried through London in triumph by the Guards and the Household Brigade. And Pitt, the greatest—and, in a certain sense, the only—British statesman who has ever managed people, parliament, government, navy, and army, all together, in a worldwide Imperial war—Pitt, the eagle-eyed and lion-hearted, at once marked Wolfe down again for higher promotion and, this time, for the command of an army of his own. And ever since the Empire Year of 1759 the world has known that Pitt was right.

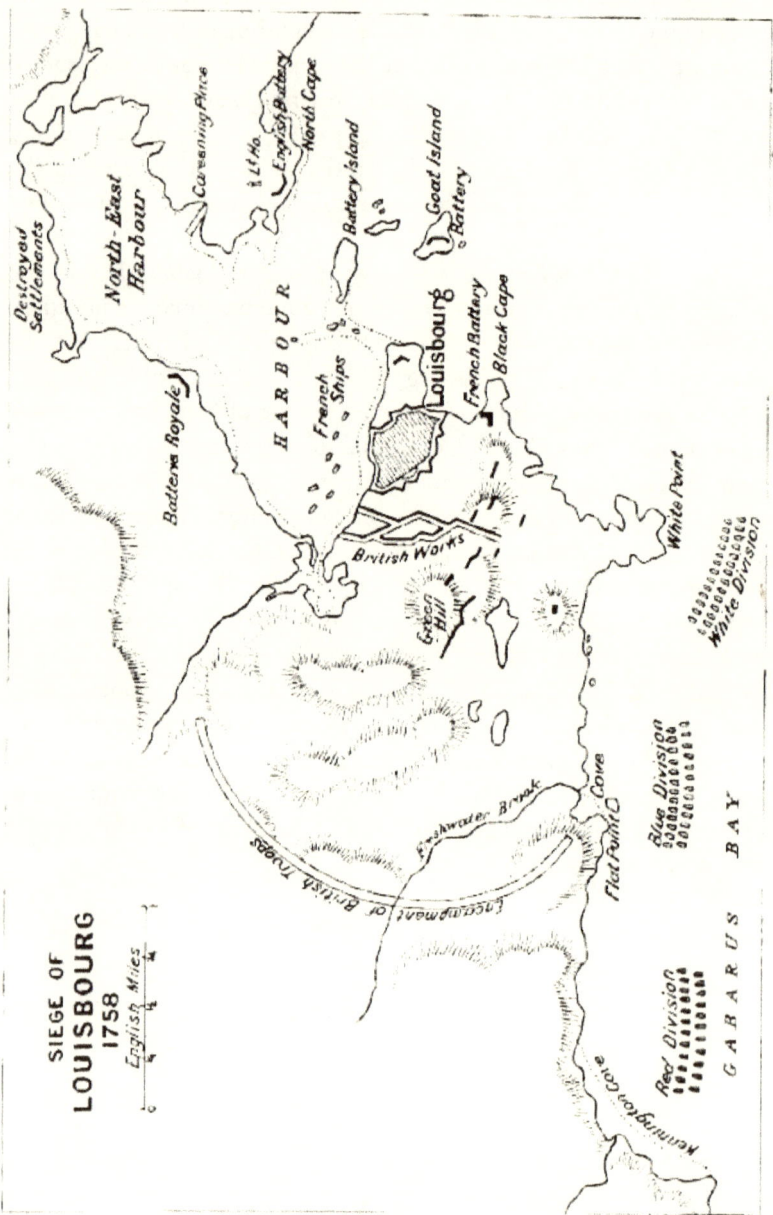

SIEGE OF
LOUISBOURG
1758

English Miles

Destroyed Settlements

North-East Harbour

Careening Place

Lt Ho

English Battery

North Cape

Battery Island

Goat Island Battery

Batterie Royale

HARBOUR

French Ships

Louisbourg

French Battery

Black Cape

British Works

Green Hill

White Point

Encampment of British Troops

Freshwater Brook

Flat Point Cove

White Division

Blue Division

GARARUS BAY

Kennington Cove

Red Division

CHAPTER 6

Quebec 1759

In October 1758 Wolfe sailed from Halifax for England with Boscawen and very nearly saw a naval battle off Land's End with the French fleet returning to France from Quebec. The enemy, however, slipped away in the dark. On November 1 he landed at Portsmouth. He had been made full colonel of a new regiment, the 67th Foot (Hampshires), and before going home to London he set off to see it at Salisbury.[1] Wolfe's old regiment, the 20th (Lancashire Fusiliers), was now in Germany, fighting under the command of Prince Ferdinand of Brunswick, and was soon to win more laurels at Minden, the first of the three great British victories of 1759—Minden, Quebec, and Quiberon.

Though far from well, Wolfe was as keen as ever about anything that could possibly make him fit for command. He picked out the best officers with a sure eye: generals and colonels, like Carleton; captains; like Delaune, a man made for the campaigns in Canada, who, as we shall see later, led the 'Forlorn Hope' up the Heights of Abraham. Wolfe had also noted in a third member of the great Howe family a born leader of light infantry for Quebec. Wolfe was very strong on light infantry, and trained them to make sudden dashes with a very short but sharp surprise attack followed by a quick retreat under cover. One day at Louisbourg an officer said this reminded him of what Xenophon wrote about the Carduchians who harassed the rear of the world-famous 'Ten Thousand.' 'I had it from Xenophon' was Wolfe's reply. Like all great commanders, Wolfe knew what other great com-

---

1. Ten years later a Russian general saw this regiment at Minorca and was loud in his praise of its all-round excellence, when Wolfe's successor in the colonelcy, Sir James Campbell, at once said: 'The only merit due to me is the strictness with which I have followed the system introduced by the hero of Quebec.'

manders had done and thought, no matter to what age or nation they belonged: Greek, Roman, German, French, British, or any other.

Years before this he had recommended a young officer to study the Prussian Army Regulations and Vauban's book on Sieges. Nor did he forget to read the lives of men like Scanderbeg and Ziska, who could teach him many unusual lessons. He kept his eyes open everywhere, all his life long, on men and things and books. He recommended his friend. Captain Rickson, who was then in Halifax, to read Montesquieu's not yet famous book *The Spirit of Laws*, because it would be useful for a government official in a new country. Writing home to his mother from Louisbourg about this new country, that is, before Canada had become British, before there was much more than a single million of English-speaking people in the whole New World, and before most people on either side of the Atlantic understood what a great oversea empire meant at all, he said: 'This will sometime hence, be a vast empire, the seat of power and learning. Nature has refused them nothing, and there will grow a people out of our little spot, England, that will fill this vast space, and divide this great portion of the globe with the Spaniards, who are possessed of the other half of it.'

On arriving in England Wolfe had reported his presence to the commander-in-chief, Lord Ligonier, requesting leave of absence in order that he might visit his relatives. This was granted, and the Wolfe family met together once more and for the last time.

Though he said little about it, Wolfe must have snatched some time for Katherine Lowther, his second love, to whom he was now engaged. What had happened between him and his first love, Miss Lawson, will probably never be known. We know that his parents were opposed to his marrying her. Perhaps, too, she may not have been as much in love as he was. But, for whatever reason, they parted. Then he fell in love with beautiful Katherine Lowther, a sister to the Earl of Lonsdale and afterwards Duchess of Bolton.

Meanwhile Pitt was planning for his Empire Year of 1759, the year of Ferdinand at Minden, Wolfe at Quebec, and Hawke in Quiberon Bay. Before Pitt had taken the war in hand nearly everything had gone against the British. Though Clive had become the British hero of India in 1757, and Wolfe of Louisbourg in 1758, there had hitherto been more defeats than victories. Minorca had been lost in 1756; in America Braddock's army had been destroyed in 1755; and Montcalm had won victories at Oswego in 1756, at Fort William Henry in 1757, and at Ticonderoga in 1758. More than this, in 1759 the French were preparing fleets and armies to invade England, Ireland, and Scotland; and the British people were thinking rather of their own defence at home than of attacking the French abroad.

Pitt, however, rightly thought that vigorous attacks from the sea were the best means of defence at home. From London he looked out over the whole world: at France and her allies in the centre, at French India on his far left, and at French Canada on his far right; with the sea dividing his enemies and uniting his friends, if only he could hold its highways with the British Navy.

To carry out his plans Pitt sent a small army and a great deal of money to Frederick the Great, to help him in the middle of Europe against the Russians, Austrians, and French. At the same time he let Anson station fleets round the coast of France, so that no strong French force could get at Britain or Greater Britain, or go to help Greater France, without a fight at sea. Then, having cut off Canada from France and taken her outpost at Louisbourg, he aimed a death-blow at her very heart by sending Saunders, with a quarter of the whole British Navy, against Quebec, the stronghold of New France, where the land attack was to be made by a little army of 9,000 men under Wolfe. Even this was not the whole of Pitt's plan for the conquest of Canada. A smaller army was to be sent against the French on the Great Lakes, and a larger one, under Amherst, along the line of Lake Champlain, towards Montreal.

Pitt did a very bold thing when he took a young colonel and asked the king to make him a general and allow him to choose his own brigadiers and staff officers. It was a bold thing, because, whenever there is a position of honour to be given, the older men do not like being passed over and all the politicians who think of themselves first and their country afterwards wish to put in their own favourites. Wolfe, of course, had enemies. Dullards often think that men of genius are crazy, and someone had told the king that Wolfe was mad. 'Mad, is he?' said the king, remembering all the recent British defeats on land 'then I hope he'll bite some of my other generals!' Wolfe was not able to give any of his seniors his own and Lord Howe's kind of divine 'madness' during that war. But he did give a touch of it to many of his juniors; with the result that his Quebec army was better officered than any other British land force of the time.

The three brigadiers next in command to Wolfe—Monckton, Townshend, and Murray—were not chosen simply because they were all sons of peers, but because, like Howe and Boscawen, they were first-rate officers as well. Barre and Carleton were the two chief men on the staff. Each became celebrated in later days, Barre in parliament, and Carleton as both the saviour of Canada from the American attack in 1775 and the first British governor-general. Williamson, the best gunnery expert in the whole Army, commanded the artillery. The only troublesome officer was Townshend, who thought himself, and whose family and political friends thought him, at least as good a general as Wolfe, if not a better one.

But even Townshend did his duty well. The army at Halifax was supposed to be twelve thousand, but its real strength was only nine thousand. The difference was mostly due to the ravages of scurvy and camp fever, both of which, in their turn, were due to the bad food supplied by rascally contractors. The action of the officers alone saved the situation from becoming desperate. Indeed, if it had not been for what the officers did for their men in the way of buying better food, at great cost, out of their own not well-filled pockets, there might have been no army at all to greet Wolfe on his arrival in America.

The fleet was the greatest that had ever sailed across the seas. It included one-quarter of the whole Royal Navy. There were 49 men-of-war manned by 14,000 sailors and marines. There were also more than 200 vessels—transports, store ships, provision ships, etc.—manned by about 7,000 merchant seamen. Thus there were at least twice as many sailors as soldiers at the taking of Quebec. Saunders was a most capable admiral. He had been flag-lieutenant during Anson's famous voyage round the world; then Hawke's best fighting captain during the war in which Wolfe was learning his work at Dettingen and Laffeldt; and then Hawke's second-in-command of the 'cargo of courage' sent out after Byng's disgrace at Minorca. After Quebec he crowned his fine career by being one of the best first lords of the Admiralty that ever ruled the navy. Durell, his next in command, was slower than Amherst; and Amherst never made a short cut in his life, even to certain success. Holmes, the third admiral, was thoroughly efficient.

Hood, a still better admiral than any of those at Quebec, afterwards served under Holmes, and Nelson under Hood; which links Trafalgar with Quebec. But a still closer link with 'mighty Nelson' was Jervis, who took charge of Wolfe's personal belongings at Quebec the night before the battle and many years later became Nelson's commander-in-chief. Another Quebec captain who afterwards became a great admiral was Hughes, famous for his fights in India. But the man whose subsequent fame in the world at large eclipsed that of any other in this fleet was Captain Cook, who made the first good charts of Canadian waters some years before he became a great explorer in the far Pacific.

There was a busy scene at Portsmouth on February 17, when Saunders and Wolfe sailed in the flagship H.M.S. *Neptune*, of 90 guns and a crew of 750 men. She was one of the well-known old 'three-deckers,' those 'wooden walls of England' that kept the Empire safe while it was growing up. The guard of red-coated marines presented arms, and the hundreds of bluejackets were all in their places as the two commanders stepped on board. The naval officers on the quarter-deck were very spick and span in their black three-cornered hats, white wigs, long, bright blue, gold-laced coats, white waistcoats and breeches and stockings, and gold-buckled shoes. The idea of having naval uniforms of blue and white and gold—the same colours that are worn today—came from the king's seeing the pretty Duchess of Bedford in a blue-and-white riding-habit, which so charmed him that he swore he would make the officers wear the same colours for the uniforms just then being newly tried. This was when the Duke of Bedford was first lord of the Admiralty, some years before Pitt's great expedition against Quebec.

The sailors were also in blue and white; but they were not so spick and span as the officers. They were a very rough-and-ready-looking lot. They wore small, soft, three-cornered black hats, bright blue jackets, open enough to show their coarse white shirts, and coarse white duck trousers. They had shoes without stockings on shore, and only bare feet on board. They carried cutlasses and pistols, and wore their hair in pigtails. They would be a surprising sight to modern eyes. But not so much soas the women! Ships and regiments in those days always had a certain number of women for washing and mending the clothes. There was one woman to about every twenty men. They drew pay and were under regular orders just like the soldiers and sailors. Sometimes they gave a willing hand in action, helping the 'powder-monkeys'—boys who had to pass the powder from the barrels to the gunners—or even taking part in a siege, as at Louisbourg.

The voyage to Halifax was long, rough, and cold, and Wolfe was sea-sick as ever. Strangely enough, these ships coming out to the conquest of Canada under St George's cross made land on St George's Day near the place where Cabot had raised St George's cross over Canadian soil before Columbus had set foot on the mainland of America. But though April 23 might be a day of good omen, it was a very bleak one that year off Cape Breton, where ice was packed for miles and miles along the coast. On the 30th the fleet entered Halifax. Slow old Durell was hurried off on May 5 with eight men-of-war and seven hundred soldiers under Carleton to try to stop any French ships from getting up to Quebec. Carleton was to go ashore at Isle-aux-Coudres, an island commanding the channel sixty miles below Quebec, and mark out a passage for the fleet through the 'Traverse' at the lower end of the island of Orleans, thirty miles higher up.

On the 13th Saunders sailed for Louisbourg, where the whole expedition was to meet and get ready. Here Wolfe spent the rest of May, working every day and all day. His army, with the exception of nine hundred American rangers, consisted of seasoned British regulars, with all the weaklings left behind; and it did his heart good to see them on parade. There was the 15th, whose officers still wear a line of black braid on their uniforms in mourning for his death. The 15th and five other regiments—the 28th, 43rd, 47th, 48th, and 58th—were English. But the 35th had been forty years in Ireland, and was Irish to a man.

The whole seven regiments were dressed very much alike: three-cornered, stiff black hats with black cockades, white wigs, long-tailed red coats turned back with blue or white in front, where they were fastened only at the neck, white breeches, and long white gaiters coming over the knee. A very different corps was the 78th, or 'Fraser's,' Highlanders, one of the regiments Wolfe first recommended and Pitt first raised. Only fourteen years before the Quebec campaign these same Highlanders had joined Prince Charlie, the Young Pretender, in the famous '45.' They were mostly Roman Catholics, which accounts for the way they intermarried with the French Canadians after the conquest. They had been fighting for the Stuarts against King George, and Wolfe, as we have seen, had himself fought against them at Culloden. Yet here they were now, under Wolfe, serving King George. They knew that the Stuart cause was lost forever; and all of them, chiefs and followers alike, loved the noble profession of arms.

The Highlanders then wore 'bonnets' like a high tam-o'-shanter, with one white curly feather on the left side. Their red coats were faced with yellow, and they wore the Fraser plaid hung from the shoulders and caught up, loopwise, on both hips. Their kilts were very short and not pleated. Badger sporrans, showing the head in the middle, red-and-white-diced hose, and buckled brogues completed their wild but martial dress, which was well set off by the dirks and claymores that swung to the stride of the mountaineer.

Each regiment had one company of grenadiers, picked out for their size, strength, and steadiness, and one company of light infantry, picked out for their quickness and good marksmanship. Sometimes all the grenadier companies would be put together in a separate battalion. The same thing was often done with the light infantry companies, which were then led by Colonel Howe. Wolfe had also made up a small three-company battalion of picked grenadiers from the five regiments that were being left behind at Louisbourg to guard the Maritime Provinces. This little battalion became famous at Quebec as the 'Louisbourg Grenadiers.' The grenadiers all wore red and white, like the rest, except that their coats were buttoned up the whole way, and instead of the three-cornered hats they wore high ones like a bishop's mitre. The artillery wore blue-grey coats turned back with red, yellow braid, and half-moon-shaped black hats, with the points down towards their shoulders.

The only remaining regiment is of much greater interest in connection with a Canadian campaign. It was the 60th Foot, then called the Royal Americans, afterwards the Sixtieth Rifles or 'Old Sixtieth,' and now the King's Royal Rifle Corps. It was the first regiment of regulars ever raised in Greater Britain, and the first to introduce the rifle-green uniform now known all over the Empire, especially in Canada, where all rifle regiments still follow 'the 60th's' lead so far as that is possible. Many of its officers and men who returned from the conquest of Canada to their homes in the British colonies were destined to move on to Canada with their families as United Empire Loyalists. This was their first war; and they did so well in it that Wolfe gave them the rifleman's motto they still bear in token of their smartness and dash—*Celer et Audax*. Unfortunately they did not then wear the famous 'rifle green' but the ordinary red.

Unfortunately, too, the rifleman's green has no connection with the 'green jackets of American backwoodsmen in the middle of the eighteenth century.' The backwoodsmen were not dressed in green as a rule, and they never formed any considerable part of the regiment at any time. The first green uniform came in with the new 5th battalion in 1797; and the old 2nd and 3rd battalions, which fought under Wolfe, did not adopt it till 1815. It was not even of British origin, but an imitation of a German hussar uniform which was itself an imitation of one worn by the Hungarians, who have the senior hussars of the world. But though Wolfe's Royal Americans did not wear the rifle green, and though their coats and waistcoats were of common red, their uniforms differed from those of all other regiments at Quebec in several particulars.

The most remarkable difference was the absence of lace, an absence specially authorized only for this corps, and then only in view of special service and many bush fights in America. The double-breasted coats were made to button across, except at the top, where the lapels turned back, like the cuffs and coat-tails. All these 'turnbacks' and the breeches were blue. The very long gaiters, the waist and cross belts, the neckerchief and hat piping were white. Wearing this distinctively plain uniform, and led by their buglers and drummers in scarlet and gold, like state trumpeters, the Royal Americans could not, even at a distance, be mistaken for any other regiment.

On June 6 Saunders and Wolfe sailed for Quebec with a hundred and forty-one ships. Wolfe's work in getting his army safely off being over, he sat down alone in his cabin to make his will. His first thought was for Katherine Lowther, his *fiancee*, who was to have her own miniature portrait, which he carried with him, set in jewels and given back to her. Warde, Howe, and Carleton were each remembered. He left all the residue of his estate to 'my good mother,' his father having just died. More than a third of the whole will was taken up with providing for his servants. No wonder he was called 'the soldier's friend.'

There was a thrilling scene at Louisbourg as regiment after regiment marched down to the shore, with drums beating, bugles sounding, and colours flying. Each night, after drinking the king's health, they had drunk another toast—'British colours on every French fort, port, and garrison in North America.' Now here they were, the pick of the Army and Navy, off with Wolfe to raise those colours over Quebec, the most important military point on the whole continent. On they sailed, all together, till they reached the Saguenay, a hundred and twenty miles below Quebec.

Here, on the afternoon of June 20, the sun shone down on a sight such as the New World had never seen before, and has never seen again. The river narrows opposite the Saguenay and is full of shoals and islands; so this was the last day the whole one hundred and forty-one vessels sailed together, in their three divisions, under those three ensigns—'The Red, White, and Blue'—which have made the British Navy loved, feared, and famous round the seven seas. What a sight it was! Thousands and thousands of soldiers and sailors crowded those scores and scores of high-decked ships; while hundreds and hundreds of swelling sails gleamed white against the sun, across the twenty miles of blue St Lawrence.

Wolfe, however, was not there to see it. He had gone forward the day before. A dispatch-boat had come down from Durell to say that, in spite of his advanced squadron, Bougainville, Montcalm's ablest brigadier, had slipped through with twenty-three ships from France, bringing out a few men and a good deal of ammunition, stores, and food. This gave Quebec some sorely needed help. Besides, Montcalm had found out Pitt's plan; and nobody knew where the only free French fleet was now. It had wintered in the West Indies. But had it sailed for France or the St Lawrence? At the first streak of dawn on the 23rd Durell's lookout off Isle-aux-Coudres reported many ships coming up the river under a press of sail. Could the French West Indian fleet have slipped in ahead of Saunders, as Bougainville had slipped in ahead of Durell himself? There was a tense moment on board of Durell's squadron and in Carleton's camp, in the pale, grey light of early morning, as the bugles sounded, the boatswains blew their whistles and roared their orders, and all hands came tumbling up from below and ran to battle quarters with a rush of swift bare feet. But the incoming vanship made the private British signal, and both sides knew that all was well.

For a whole week the great fleet of one hundred and forty-one ships worked their way through the narrow channel between Isle-aux-Coudres and the north shore, and then dared the dangers of the Traverse, below the island of Orleans, where the French had never passed more than one ship at a time, and that only with the greatest caution. The British went through quite easily, without a single accident. In two days the great Captain Cook had sounded and marked out the channel better than the French had in a hundred and fifty years; and so thoroughly was his work done that the British officers could handle their vessels in these French waters better without than with the French pilots. Old Captain Killick took the *Goodwill* through himself, just next ahead of the *Richmond*, on board of which was Wolfe. The captured French pilot in the *Goodwill* was sure she would be lost if she did not go slow and take more care. But Killick laughed at him and said: 'Damn me, but I'll convince you an Englishman can go where a Frenchman daren't show his nose!' And he did.

On June 26 Wolfe arrived at the west end of the island of Orleans, in full view of Quebec. The twenty days' voyage from Louisbourg had ended and the twelve weeks' siege had begun. At this point we must take the map and never put it aside till the final battle is over. A whole book could not possibly make Wolfe's work plain to any one without the map. But with the map we can easily follow every move in this, the greatest crisis in both Wolfe's career and Canada's history.

What Wolfe saw and found out was enough to daunt any general. He had a very good army, but it was small. He could count upon the help of a mighty fleet, but even British fleets cannot climb hills or make an enemy come down and fight. Montcalm, however, was weakened by many things. The governor, Vaudreuil, was a vain, fussy, and spiteful fool, with power enough to thwart Montcalm at every turn. The *intendant*, Bigot, was the greatest knave ever seen in Canada, and the head of a gang of official thieves who robbed the country and the wretched French Canadians right and left. The French army, all together, numbered nearly seventeen thousand, almost twice Wolfe's own; but the bulk of it was militia, half starved and badly armed. Both Vaudreuil and Bigot could and did interfere disastrously with the five different forces that should have been made into one army under Montcalm alone—the French regulars, the Canadian regulars, the Canadian militia, the French sailors ashore, and the Indians.

Montcalm had one great advantage over Wolfe. He was not expected to fight or manoeuvre in the open field. His duty was not to drive Wolfe away, or even to keep Amherst out of Canada. All he had to do was to hold Quebec throughout the summer. The autumn would force the British fleet to leave for ice-free waters. Then, if Quebec could only be held, a change in the fortunes of war, or a treaty of peace, might still keep Canada in French hands. Wolfe had either to tempt Montcalm out of Quebec or get into it himself; and he soon realized that he would have to do this with the help of Saunders alone; for Amherst in the south was crawling forward towards Montreal so slowly that no aid from him could be expected.

Montcalm's position certainly looked secure for the summer. His left flank was guarded by the Montmorency, a swift river that could be forded only by a few men at a time in a narrow place, some miles up, where the dense bush would give every chance to his Indians and Canadians. His centre was guarded by entrenchments running from the Montmorency to the St Charles, six miles of ground, rising higher and higher towards Montmorency, all of it defended by the best troops and the bulk of the army, and none of it having an inch of cover for an enemy in front. The mouth of the St Charles was blocked by booms and batteries. Quebec is a natural fortress; and above Quebec the high, steep cliffs stretched for miles and miles. These cliffs could be climbed by a few men in several places; but nowhere by a whole army, if any defenders were there in force; and the British fleet could not land an army without being seen soon enough to draw plenty of defenders to the same spot.

Forty miles above Quebec the St Lawrence channel narrows to only a quarter of a mile, and the down current becomes very swift indeed. Above this channel was the small French fleet, which could stop a much larger one trying to get up, or could even block most of the fairway by sinking some of its own ships. Besides all these defences of man and nature the French had floating batteries along the north shore. They also held the Levis Heights on the south shore, opposite Quebec, so that ships crowded with helpless infantry could not, without terrible risk, run through the intervening narrows, barely a thousand yards wide.

A gale blowing down-stream was the first trouble for the British fleet. Many of the transports broke loose and a good deal of damage was done to small vessels and boats. Next night a greater danger threatened, when the ebb-tide, running five miles an hour, brought down seven French fireships, which suddenly burst into flame as they rounded the Point of Levy. There was a display of devil's fireworks such as few men have ever seen or could imagine. Sizzling, crackling, and roaring, the blinding flames leaped into the jet-black sky, lighting up the camps of both armies, where thousands of soldiers watched these engines of death sweep down on the fleet. Each of the seven ships was full of mines, blowing up and hurling shot and shell in all directions.

The crowded mass of British vessels seemed doomed to destruction. But the first spurt of fire had hardly been noticed before the men in the guard boats began to row to the rescue. Swinging the grappling-hooks round at arm's length, as if they were heaving the lead, the bluejackets made the fireships fast, the officers shouted, 'Give way!' and presently the whole infernal flotilla was safely stranded. But it was a close thing and very hot work, as one of the happy-go-lucky Jack tars said with more force than grace, when he called out to the boat beside him: 'Hullo, mate! Did you ever take hell in tow before?'

Vaudreuil now made Montcalm, who was under his orders, withdraw the men from the Levis Heights, and thus abandon the whole of the south shore in front of Quebec. Wolfe, delighted, at once occupied the same place, with half his army and most of his guns. Then he seized the far side of the Montmorency and made his main camp

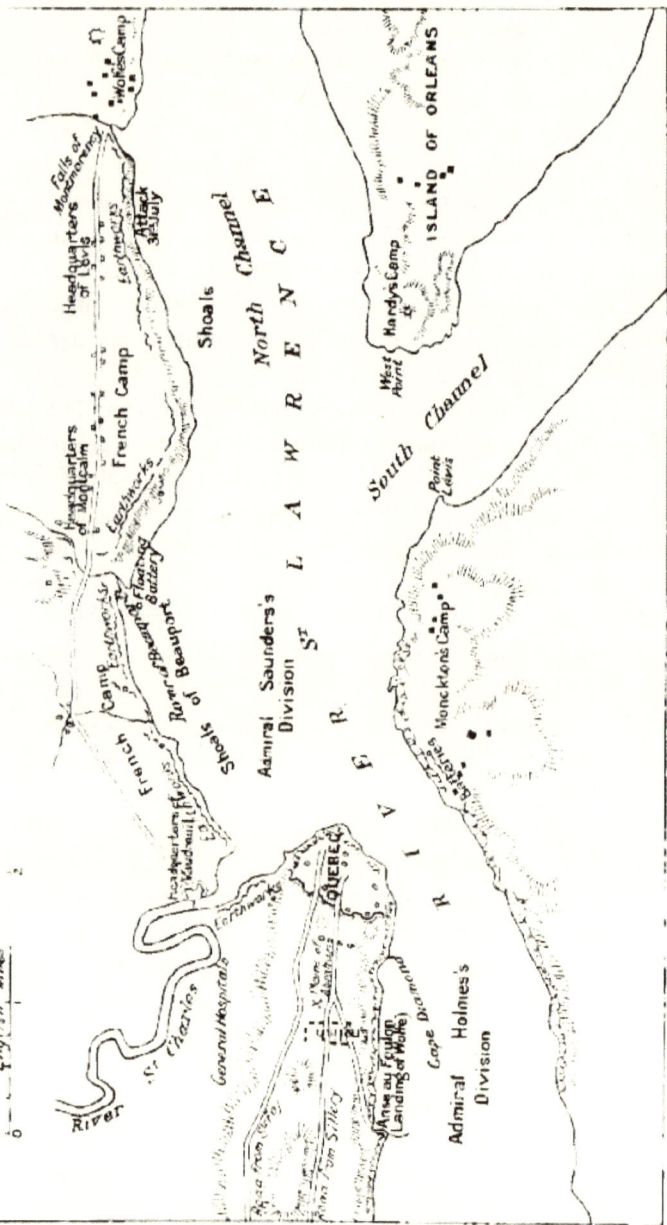

SIEGE OF QUEBEC
1759

English Miles

River St Charles

River St Lawrence

QUEBEC

General Hospital

Headquarters of Vaudreuil

French Camp

Northwork

Headquarters of Montcalm

French Camp

Earthworks

River Beauport

Shoals of Beauport

Floating Battery

Shoals

North Channel

Headquarters of Wolfe

Falls of Montmorency

Earthworks

Attack 31 July

Admiral Saunders's Division

South Channel

West Point

ISLAND OF ORLEANS

Hardy's Camp

Point Lewis

Monckton's Camp

Cape Diamond

Anse au Foulon
(Landing of Wolfe)

Admiral Holmes's
Division

there, without, however, removing his hospitals and stores from his camp on the island of Orleans. So he now had three camps, not divided, but joined together, by the St Lawrence, where the fleet could move about between them in spite of anything the French could do. He then marched up the Montmorency to the fords, to try the French strength there, and to find out if he could cross the river, march down the open ground behind Montcalm, and attack him from the rear. But he was repulsed at the first attempt, and saw that he could do no better at a second. Meanwhile his Levis batteries began a bombardment which lasted two months and reduced Quebec to ruins.

Yet he seemed as far off as ever from capturing the city. Battering down the houses of Quebec brought him no nearer to his object, while Montcalm's main body still stood securely in its entrenchments down at Beauport. Wolfe now felt he must try something decisive, even if desperate; and he planned an attack by land and water on the French left. Both French and British were hard at work on July 31. In the morning Wolfe sent one regiment marching up the Montmorency, as if to try the fords again, and another, also in full view of the French, up along the St Lawrence from the Levis batteries, as if it was to be taken over by the ships to the north shore above Quebec.

Meanwhile Monckton's brigade was starting from the Point of Levy in row-boats, the *Centurion* was sailing down to the mouth of the Montmorency, two armed transports were being purposely run ashore on the beach at the top of the tide, and the *Pembroke, Trent, Lowestoff,* and *Racehorse* were taking up positions to cover the boats. The men-of-war and Wolfe's batteries at Montmorency then opened fire on the point he wished to attack; and both of them kept it up for eight hours, from ten till six. All this time the Levis batteries were doing their utmost against Quebec. But Montcalm was not to be deceived. He saw that Wolfe intended to storm the entrenchments at the point at which the cannon were firing, and he kept the best of his army ready to defend it.

Wolfe and the Louisbourg Grenadiers were in the two armed transports when they grounded at ten o'clock. To his disgust and to Captain Cook's surprise both vessels stuck fast in the mud nearly half a mile from shore. This made the grenadiers' muskets useless against the advanced French redoubt, which stood at high-water mark, and which overmatched the transports, because both of these had grounded in such a way that they could not bring their guns to bear in reply. The stranded vessels soon became a death-trap. Wolfe's cane was knocked out of his hand by a cannon ball. Shells were bursting over the deck, smashing the masts to pieces and sending splinters of wood and iron flying about among the helpless grenadiers and gunners. There was nothing to do but order the men back to the boats and wait. The tide was not low till four.

The weather was scorchingly hot. A thunderstorm was brewing. The redoubt could not be taken. The transports were a failure. And every move had to be made in full view of the watchful Montcalm, whose entrenchments at this point were on the top of a grassy hill nearly two hundred feet above the muddy beach. But Wolfe still thought he might succeed with the main attack at low tide, although he had not been able to prepare it at high tide. His Montmorency batteries seemed to be pitching their shells very thickly into the French, and his three brigades of infantry were all ready to act together at the right time. Accordingly, for the hottest hours of that scorching day, Monckton's men grilled in the boats while Townshend's and Murray's waited in camp. At four the tide was low and Wolfe ordered the landing to begin.

The tidal flats ran out much farther than anyone had supposed. The heavily laden boats stuck on an outer ledge and had to be cleared, shoved off, refilled with soldiers, and brought round to another place. It was now nearly six o'clock; and both sides were eager for the fray. Townshend's and Murray's brigades had forded the mouth of the Montmorency and were marching along to support the attack, when, suddenly and unexpectedly, the grenadiers spoiled it all! Wolfe had ordered the Louisbourg Grenadiers and the ten other grenadier companies of the army to form up and rush the redoubt. But, what with the cheering of the sailors as they landed the rest of Monckton's men, and their own eagerness to come to close quarters at once, the Louisbourg men suddenly lost their heads and charged before everything was ready. The rest followed them pell-mell; and in less than five minutes the redoubt was swarming with excited grenadiers, while the French who had held it were clambering up the grassy hill into the safer entrenchments.

The redoubt was certainly no place to stay in. It had no shelter towards its rear; and dozens of French cannon and thousands of French muskets were firing into it from the heights. An immediate retirement was the only proper course. But there was no holding the men now. They broke into another mad charge, straight at the hill. As they reached it, amid a storm of musket balls and grape-shot, the heavens joined in with a terrific storm of their own. The rain burst in a perfect deluge; and the hill became almost impossible to climb, even if there had been no enemy pouring death-showers of fire from the top. When Wolfe saw what was happening he immediately sent officers running after the grenadiers to make them come back from the redoubt, and these officers now passed the word to retire at once. This time the grenadiers, all that were left of them, obeyed. Their two mad rushes had not lasted a quarter of an hour. Yet nearly half of the thousand men they started with were lying dead or wounded on that fatal ground.

Wolfe now saw that he was hopelessly beaten and that there was not a minute to lose in getting away. The boats could take only Monckton's men; and the rising tide would soon cut off Townshend's and Murray's from their camp beyond the mouth of the Montmorency. The two stranded transports, from which he had hoped so much that morning, were set on fire; and, under cover of their smoke and of the curtain of torrential rain, Monckton's crestfallen men got into their boats once more. Townshend's and Murray's brigades, enraged at not being brought into action, turned to march back by the way they had come so eagerly only an hour before. They moved off in perfect order; but, as they left the battlefield, they waved their hats in defiance at the jeering Frenchmen, challenging them to come down and fight it out with bayonets hand to hand.

Many gallant deeds were done that afternoon; but none more gallant than those of Captain Ochterloney and Lieutenant Peyton, both grenadier officers in the Royal Americans. Ochterloney had just been wounded in a duel; but he said his country's honour came before his own, and, sick and wounded as he was, he spent those panting hours in the boats without a murmur and did all he could to form his men up under fire. In the second charge he fell, shot through the lungs, with Peyton beside him, shot through the leg. When Wolfe called the grenadiers back a rescue party wanted to carry off both officers, to save them from the scalping-knife. But Ochterloney said he would never leave the field after such a defeat; and Peyton said he would never leave his captain.

Presently a Canadian regular came up with two Indians, grabbed Ochterloney's watch, sword and money, and left the Indians to finish him. One of these savages clubbed him with a musket, while the other shot him in the chest and dashed in with a scalping-knife. In the meantime, Peyton crawled on his hands and knees to a double-barrelled musket and shot one Indian dead, but missed the other. This savage now left Ochterloney, picked up a bayonet and rushed at Peyton, who drew his dagger. A terrible life-and-death fight followed; but Peyton at last got a good point well driven home, straight through the Indian's heart. A whole scalping party now appeared. Ochterloney was apparently dead, and Peyton was too exhausted to fight any more. But, at this very moment, another British party came back for the rest of the wounded and carried Peyton off to the boats.

Then the Indians came back to scalp Ochterloney. By this time, however, some French regulars had come down, and one of them, finding Ochterloney still alive, drove off the Indians at the point of the bayonet, secured help, and carried him up the hill. Montcalm had him carefully taken into the General Hospital, where he was tenderly nursed by the nuns. Two days after he had been rescued, a French officer came out for his clothes and other effects. Wolfe then sent in twenty guineas for his rescuer, with a promise that, in return for the kindness shown to Ochterloney, the General Hospital would be specially protected if the British took Quebec. Towards the end of August Ochterloney died; and both sides ceased firing while a French captain came out to report his death and return his effects.

This was by no means the only time the two enemies treated each other like friends. A party of French ladies were among the prisoners brought in to Wolfe one day; and they certainly had no cause to complain of him. He gave them a dinner, at which he charmed them all by telling them about his visit to Paris. The next morning he sent them into Quebec with his *aide-de-camp* under a flag of truce. Another time the French officers sent him a kind of wine which was not to be had in the British camp, and he sent them some not to be had in their own.

But the stern work of war went on and on, though the weary month of August did not seem to bring victory any closer than disastrous July. Wolfe knew that September was to be the end of the campaign, the now-or-never of his whole career. And, knowing this, he set to work—head and heart and soul—on making the plan that brought him victory, death, and everlasting fame.

CHAPTER 7

The Plains of Abraham - September 13, 1759

On August 19 an *aide-de-camp* came out of the farmhouse at Montmorency which served as the headquarters of the British army to say that Wolfe was too ill to rise from his bed. The bad news spread like wildfire through the camp and fleet, and soon became known among the French. A week passed; but Wolfe was no better. Tossing about on his bed in a fever, he thought bitterly of his double defeat, of the critical month of September, of the grim strength of Quebec, formed by nature for a stronghold, and then—worse still—of his own weak body, which made him most helpless just when he should have been most fit for his duty.

Feeling that he could no longer lead in person, he dictated a letter to the brigadiers, sent them the secret instructions he had received from Pitt and the king, and asked them to think over his three new plans for attacking Montcalm at Beauport. They wrote back to say they thought the defeats at the upper fords of the Montmorency and at the heights facing the St Lawrence showed that the French could not be beaten by attacking the Beauport lines again, no matter from what side the attack was made. They then gave him a plan of their own, which was, to convey the army up the St Lawrence and fight their way ashore somewhere between Cap Rouge, nine miles above Quebec, and Pointe-aux-Trembles, twenty-two miles above. They argued that, by making a landing there, the British could cut off Montcalm's communications with Three Rivers and Montreal, from which his army drew its supplies. Wolfe's letter was dictated from his bed of sickness on the 26th. The brigadiers answered him on the 29th. Saunders talked it all over with him on the 31st. Before this the fate of Canada had been an affair of weeks. Now it was a matter of days; for the morrow would dawn on the very last possible month of the siege—September.

After his talk with Saunders Wolfe wrote his last letter home to his mother, telling her of his desperate plight:

> The enemy puts nothing to risk, and I can't in conscience put the whole army to risk. My antagonist has wisely shut himself up in inaccessible entrenchments, so that I can't get at him without spilling a torrent of blood, and that perhaps to little purpose. The Marquis de Montcalm is at the head of a great number of bad soldiers and I am at the head of a small number of good ones, that wish for nothing so much as to fight him; but the wary old fellow avoids an action, doubtful of the behaviour of his army. People must be of the profession to understand the disadvantages and difficulties we labour under, arising from the uncommon natural strength of the country.

On September 2 he wrote his last letter to Pitt. He had asked the doctors to 'patch him up,' saying that if they could make him fit for duty for only the next few days they need not trouble about what might happen to him afterwards. Their 'patching up' certainly cleared his fevered brain, for this letter was a masterly account of the whole siege and the plans just laid to bring it to an end. The style was so good, indeed, that Charles Townshend said his brother George must have been the real author, and that Wolfe, whom he dubbed 'a fiery-headed fellow, only fit for fighting,' could not have done any more than sign his name. But when George Townshend's own official letter about the battle in which Wolfe fell was also published, and was found to be much less effective than Wolfe's, Selwyn went up to Charles Townshend and said: 'Look here, Charles, if your brother wrote Wolfe's letter, who the devil wrote your brother's?'

Wolfe did not try to hide anything from Pitt. He told him plainly about the two defeats and the terrible difficulties in the way of winning any victory. The whole letter is too long for quotation, and odd scraps from it give no idea of Wolfe's lucid style. But here are a few which tell the gist of the story:

> I found myself so ill, and am still so weak, that I begged the generals to consult together. They are all of opinion, that, as more ships and provisions are now got above the town, they should try, by conveying up five thousand men, to draw the

enemy from his present position and bring him to an action. I have acquiesced in their proposal, and we are preparing to put it into execution. The admiral will readily join in any measure for the public service. There is such a choice of difficulties that I own myself at a loss how to determine. The affairs of Great Britain I know require the most vigorous measures. You may be sure that the small part of the campaign which remains shall be employed, as far as I am able, for the honour of His Majesty and the interest of the nation. I am sure of being well seconded by the admirals and generals; happy if our efforts here can contribute to the success of His Majesty's arms in any other part of America.

On the 31st, the day he wrote to his mother and had his long talk with Saunders, Wolfe began to send his guns and stores away from the Montmorency camp. Carleton managed the removal very cleverly; and on September 3 only the five thousand infantry who were to go up the St Lawrence were left there. Wolfe tried to tempt Montcalm to attack him. But Montcalm knew better; and half suspected that Wolfe himself might make another attack on the Beauport lines. When everything was ready, all the men at the Point of Levy who could be spared put off in boats and rowed over towards Beauport, just as Monckton's men had done on the disastrous last day of July.

At the same time the main division of the fleet, under Saunders, made as if to support these boats, while the Levis batteries thundered against Quebec. Carleton gave the signal from the beach at Montmorency when the tide was high; and the whole five thousand infantry marched down the hill, got into their boats, and rowed over to where the other boats were waiting. The French now prepared to defend themselves at once. But as the two divisions of boats came together, they both rowed off through the gaps between the men-of-war. Wolfe's army had broken camp and got safely away, right under the noses of the French, without the loss of a single man.

A whole week, from September 3 to 10, was then taken up with trying to see how the brigadiers' plan could be carried out.

This plan was good, as far as it went. An army is even harder to supply than a town would be if the town was taken up bodily and moved about the country. An army makes no supplies itself, but uses up a great deal. It must have food, clothing, arms, ammunition, stores of all kinds, and everything else it needs to keep it fit for action. So it must always keep what are called 'communications' with the places from which it gets these supplies. Now, Wolfe's and Montcalm's armies were both supplied along the St Lawrence, Wolfe's from below Quebec and Montcalm's from above. But Wolfe had no trouble about the safety of his own 'communications,' since they were managed and protected by the fleet.

Even before he first saw Quebec, a convoy of supply ships had sailed from the Maritime Provinces for his army under the charge of a man-of-war. And so it went on all through the siege. Including forty-nine men-of-war, no less than 277 British vessels sailed up to Quebec during this campaign; and not one of them was lost on the way, though the St Lawrence had then no lighthouses, buoys, or other aids to navigation, as it has now, and though the British officers themselves were compelled to take the ships through the worst places in these foreign and little-known waters. The result was that there were abundant supplies for the British army the whole time, thanks to the fleet.

But Montcalm was in a very different plight. Since the previous autumn, when Wolfe and Hardy had laid waste the coast of Gaspe, the supply of sea-fish had almost failed. Now the whole country below Quebec had been cut off by the fleet, while most of the country round Quebec was being laid waste by the army. Wolfe's orders were that no man, woman, or child was to be touched, nor any house or other buildings burnt, if his own men were not attacked. But if the men of the country fired at his soldiers they were to be shot down, and everything they had was to be destroyed. Of course, women and children were strictly protected, under all circumstances, and no just complaint was ever made against the British for hurting a single one. But as the men persisted in firing, the British fired back and destroyed the farms where the firing took place, on the fair-play principle that it is right to destroy whatever is used to destroy you.

It thus happened that, except at a few little villages where the men had not fired on the soldiers, the country all round Quebec was like a desert, as far as supplies for the French were concerned. The only way to obtain anything for their camp was by bringing it down the St Lawrence from Montreal, Sorel, and Three Rivers. French vessels would come down as far as they dared and then send the supplies on in barges, which kept close in under the north shore above Quebec, where the French outposts and batteries protected them from the British men-of-war that were pushing higher and higher up the river.

Some supplies were brought in by land after they were put ashore above the highest British vessels. But as a hundred tons came far more easily by water than one ton by land, it is not hard to see that Montcalm's men could not hold out long if the St Lawrence near Quebec was closed to supplies.

Wolfe, Montcalm, the brigadiers, and everyone else on both sides knew this perfectly well. But, as it was now September, the fleet could not go far up the much more difficult channel towards Montreal. If it did, and took Wolfe's army with it, the few French men-of-war might dispute the passage, and some sunken ships might block the way, at all events for a time. Besides, the French were preparing to repulse any landing up the river, between Cap Rouge, nine miles above Quebec, and Deschambault, forty miles above; and with good prospect of success, because the country favoured their irregulars. Moreover, if Wolfe should land many miles up, Montcalm might still hold out far down in Quebec for the few days remaining till October. If, on the other hand, the fleet went up and left Wolfe's men behind, Montcalm would be safer than ever at Beauport and Quebec; because, how could Wolfe reach him without a fleet when he had failed to reach him with one?

The life-and-death question for Wolfe was how to land close enough above Quebec and soon enough in September to make Montcalm fight it out on even terms and in the open field.

The brigadiers' plan of landing high up seemed all right till they tried to work it out. Then they found troubles in plenty. There were several places for them to land between Cap Rouge, nine miles above Quebec, and Pointe-aux-Trembles, thirteen miles higher still. Ever since July 18 British vessels had been passing to and fro above Quebec; and in August, Murray, under the guard of Holmes's squadron, had tried his brigade against Pointe-aux-Trembles, where he was beaten back, and at Deschambault, twenty miles farther up, where he took some prisoners and burnt some supplies. To ward off further and perhaps more serious attacks from this quarter, Montcalm had been keeping Bougainville on the lookout, especially round Pointe-aux-Trembles, for several weeks before the brigadiers arranged their plan.

Bougainville now had 2,000 infantry, all the mounted men—nearly 300—and all the best Indian and Canadian scouts, along the thirteen miles of shore between Cap Rouge and Pointe-aux-Trembles. His land and water batteries had also been made much stronger. He and Montcalm were in close touch and could send messages to each other and get an answer back within four hours.

On the 7th Wolfe and the brigadiers had a good look at every spot round Pointe-aux-Trembles. On the 8th and 9th the brigadiers were still there; while five transports sailed past Quebec on the 8th to join Holmes, who commanded the upriver squadron. Two of Wolfe's brigades were now on board the transports with Holmes. But the whole three were needed; and this need at once entailed another difficulty. A successful landing on the north shore above Quebec could only be made under cover of the dark; and Wolfe could not bring the third brigade, under cover of night, from the island of Orleans and the Point of Levy, and land it with the other two twenty miles up the river before daylight. The tidal stream runs up barely five hours, while it runs down more than seven; and winds are mostly down.

Next, if, instead of sailing, the third brigade marched twenty miles at night across very rough country on the south shore, it would arrive later than ever. Then, only one brigade could be put ashore in boats at one time in one place, and Bougainville could collect enough men to hold it in check while he called in reinforcements at least as fast on the French side as the British could on theirs. Another thing was that the wooded country favoured the French defence and hindered the British attack. Lastly, if Wolfe and Saunders collected the whole five thousand soldiers and a still larger squadron and convoy up the river, Montcalm would see the men and ships being moved from their positions in front of his Beauport entrenchments, and would hurry to the threatened shore between Cap Rouge and Pointe-aux-Trembles almost as soon as the British, and certainly in time to reinforce Bougainville and repulse Wolfe.

The 9th was Wolfe's last Sunday. It was a cheerless, rainy day; and he almost confessed himself beaten for good, as he sat writing his last official letter to one of Pitt's friends, the Earl of Holderness. He dated it, 'On board the *Sutherland* at anchor off Cap Rouge, September 9, 1759.' He ended it with gloomy news: 'I am so far recovered as to be able to do business, but my constitution is entirely ruined, without the consolation of having done any considerable service to the state, or without any prospect of it.'

The very next day, however, he saw his chance. He stood at Etchemin, on the south shore, two miles above Quebec, and looked long and earnestly through his telescope at the Foulon road, a mile and a half away, running up to the Plains of Abraham from the Anse au Foulon, which has ever since been called Wolfe's Cove. Then he looked at the Plains themselves, especially at a spot only one mile from Quebec, where the flat and open ground formed a perfect field of battle for his well-drilled regulars. He knew the Foulon road must be fairly good, because it was the French line of communication between the Anse au Foulon and the Beauport camp. The Cove and the nearest point of the camp were only two miles and a quarter apart, as the crow flies. But between them rose the tableland of the Plains, 300 feet above the river. Thus they were screened from each other, and a surprise at the Cove might not be found out too soon at the camp.

Now, Wolfe knew that the French expected to be attacked either above Cap Rouge (up towards Pointe-aux-Trembles) or below Quebec (down in their Beauport entrenchments). He also knew that his own army thought the attack would be made above Cap Rouge. Thus the French were still very anxious about the six miles at Beauport, while both sides were keenly watching each other all over the thirteen miles above Cap Rouge. Nobody seemed to be thinking about the nine miles between Cap Rouge and Quebec, and least of all about the part nearest Quebec.

Yes, one man was thinking about it, and he never stopped thinking about it till he died. That man was Montcalm. On the 5th, when Wolfe began moving up-stream, Montcalm had sent a whole battalion to the Plains. But on the 7th, when the British generals were all at Pointe-aux-Trembles, Vaudreuil, always ready to spite Montcalm, ordered this battalion back to camp, saying, 'The British haven't got wings; they can't fly up to the Plains!' Wolfe, of course, saw that the battalion had been taken away; and he soon found out why. Vaudreuil was a great talker and could never keep a secret. Wolfe knew perfectly well that Vaudreuil and Bigot were constantly spoiling whatever Montcalm was doing, so he counted on this trouble in the French camp as he did on other facts and chances.

He now gave up all idea of his old plans against Beauport, as well as the new plan of the brigadiers, and decided on another plan of his own. It was new in one way, because he had never seen a chance of carrying it out before. But it was old in another way, because he had written to his uncle from Louisbourg on May 19, and spoken of getting up the heights four or five miles above Quebec if he could do so by surprise. Again, even so early in the siege as July 18 he had been chafing at what he called the 'coldness' of the fleet about pushing up beyond Quebec. The entry in his private diary for that day is:

The *Sutherland* and *Squirrell*, two transports, and two armed sloops passed the narrow passage between Quebec and Levy *without losing a man.*

Next day, his entry is more scathing still:

Reconnoitred the country immediately above Quebec and found that *if we had ventured the stroke that was first intended we should infallibly have succeeded.*

This shows how long he had kept the plan waiting for the chance. But it does not prove that he had missed any earlier chances through the 'coldness' of the fleet. For it is significant that he afterwards struck out *'infallibly'* and substituted *'probably'*; while it must be remembered that the *Sutherland* and her consorts formed only a very small flotilla, that they passed Quebec in the middle of a very dark night, that the St Lawrence above the town was intricate and little known, that the loss of several men-of-war might have been fatal, that the enemy's attention had not become distracted in July to anything like the same bewildering extent as it had in September, and that the intervening course of events—however disappointing in itself—certainly helped to make his plan suit the occasion far better late than soon. Moreover, in a note to Saunders in August, he had spoken about a 'desperate' plan which he could not trust his brigadiers to carry out, and which he was then too sick to carry out himself.

Now that he was 'patched up' enough for a few days, and that the chance seemed to be within his grasp, he made up his mind to strike at once. He knew that the little French post above the Anse au Foulon was commanded by one of Bigot's blackguards; Vergor, whose Canadian militiamen were as slack as their commander. He knew that the Samos battery, a little farther from Quebec, had too small a garrison, with only five guns and no means of firing them on the landward side; so that any of his men, once up the heights, could rush it from the rear. He knew the French had only a few weak posts the whole way down from Cap Rouge, and that these posts often let convoys of provision boats pass quietly at night into the Anse au Foulon. He knew that some of Montcalm's best regulars had gone to Montreal with Levis, the excellent French second-in-command, to strengthen the defence against Amherst's slow advance from Lake Champlain. He knew that Montcalm still had a total of 10,000 men between Montmorency and Quebec, as against his own attacking force of 5,000; yet he also knew that the odds of two to one were reversed in his favour so far as European regulars were concerned; for Montcalm could not now bring 3,000 French regulars into immediate action at any one spot. Finally, he knew that all the French were only half-fed, and that those with Bougainville were getting worn out by having to march across country, in a fruitless effort to keep pace with the ships of Holmes's squadron and convoy, which floated up and down with the tide.

Wolfe's plan was to keep the French alarmed more than ever at the two extreme ends of their line—Beauport below Quebec and Pointe-aux-Trembles above—and then to strike home at their undefended centre, by a surprise landing at the Anse au Foulon. Once landed, well before daylight, he could rush Vergor's post and the Samos battery, march across the Plains, and form his line of battle a mile from Quebec before Montcalm could come up in force from Beauport. Probably he could also defeat him before Bougainville could march down from some point well above Cap Rouge.

There were chances to reckon with in this plan. But so there are in all plans; and to say Wolfe took Quebec by mere luck is utter nonsense. He was one of the deepest thinkers on war who ever lived, especially on the British kind of war, by land and sea together; and he had had the preparation of a lifetime to help him in using a fleet and army that worked together like the two arms of one body. He simply made a plan which took proper account of all the facts and all the chances. Fools make lucky hits, now and then, by the merest chance. But no one except a genius can make and carry out a plan like Wolfe's, which meant at least a hundred hits running, all in the selfsame spot.

No sooner had Wolfe made his admirable plan that Monday morning, September 10, than he set all the principal officers to work out the different parts of it. But he kept the whole a secret. Nobody except himself knew more than one part, and how that one part was to be worked in at the proper time and place. Even the fact that the Anse au Foulon was to be the landing-place was kept secret till the last moment from everybody except Admiral Holmes, who made all the arrangements, and Captain Chads, the naval officer who was to lead the first boats down. The great plot thickened fast. The siege that had been an affair of weeks, and the brigadiers' plan that had been an affair of days, both gave way to a plan in which every hour was made to tell. Wolfe's seventy hours of consummate manoeuvres, by land and water, over a front of thirty miles, were followed by a battle in which the fighting of only a few minutes settled the fate of Canada for centuries.

During the whole of those momentous three days—Monday, Tuesday, and Wednesday, September 10, 11, and 12, 1759—Wolfe, Saunders, and Holmes kept the French in constant alarm about the thirteen miles *above* Cap Rouge and the six miles *below* Quebec; but gave no sign by which any immediate danger could be suspected along the nine miles between Cap Rouge and Quebec.

Saunders stayed below Quebec. On the 12th he never gave the French a minute's rest all day and night. He sent Cook and others close in towards Beauport to lay buoys, as if to mark out a landing-place for another attack like the one on July 31. It is a singular coincidence that while Cook, the great British circumnavigator of the globe, was trying to get Wolfe into Quebec, Bougainville, the great French circumnavigator, was trying to keep him out. Towards evening Saunders formed up his boats and filled them with marines, whose own red coats, seen at a distance, made them look like soldiers. He moved his fleet in at high tide and fired furiously at the entrenchments.

All night long his boatloads of men rowed up and down and kept the French on the alert. This fein tagainst Beauport was much helped by the men of Wolfe's third brigade, who remained at the island of Orleans and the Point of Levy till after dark, by a whole battalion of marines guarding the Levis batteries, and by these batteries themselves, which, meanwhile, were bombarding Quebec—again like the 31st of July. The bombardment was kept up all night and became most intense just before dawn, when Wolfe was landing two miles above.

At the other end of the French line, above Cap Rouge, Holmes had kept threatening Bougainville more and more towards Pointe-aux-Trembles, twenty miles above the Foulon. Wolfe's soldiers had kept landing on the south shore day after day; then drifting up with the tide on board the transports past Pointe-aux-Trembles; then drifting down towards Cap Rouge; and then coming back the next day to do the same thing over again. This had been going on, more or less, even before Wolfe had made his plan, and it proved very useful to him. He knew that Bougainville's men were getting quite worn out by scrambling across country, day after day, to keep up with Holmes's restless squadron and transports. He also knew that men who threw themselves down, tired out, late at night could not be collected from different places, all over their thirteen-mile beat, and brought down in the morning, fit to fight on a battlefield eight miles from the nearest of them and twenty-one from the farthest.

Montcalm was greatly troubled. He saw redcoats with Saunders opposite Beauport, redcoats at the island, redcoats at the Point of Levy, and redcoats guarding the Levis batteries. He had no means of finding out at once that the redcoats with Saunders and at the batteries were marines, and that the redcoats who really did belong to Wolfe were under orders to march off after dark that very night and join the other two brigades which were coming down the river from the squadron above Cap Rouge. He had no boats that could get through the perfect screen of the British fleet. But all that the skill of mortal man could do against these odds he did on that fatal eve of battle, as he had done for three years past, with foes in front and false friends behind. He ordered the battalion which he had sent to the Plains on the 5th, and which Vaudreuil had brought back on the 7th, 'now to go and camp at the Foulon'; that is, at the top of the road coming up from Wolfe's landing-place at the Anse au Foulon. But Vaudreuil immediately gave a counter-order and said: 'We'll see about that tomorrow.' Vaudreuil's 'tomorrow' never came.

That afternoon of the 12th, while Montcalm and Vaudreuil were at cross-purposes near the mouth of the St Charles, Wolfe was only four miles away, on the other side of the Plains, in a boat on the St Lawrence, where he was taking his last look at what he then called the Foulon and what the world now calls Wolfe's Cove. His boat was just turning to drift up in midstream, off Sillery Point, which is only half a mile above the Foulon. He wanted to examine the Cove well through his telescope at dead low tide, as he intended to land his army there at the next low tide. Close beside him sat young Robison, who was not an officer in either the army or navy, but who had come out to Canada as tutor to an admiral's son, and who had been found so good at maps that he was employed with Wolfe's engineers in making surveys and sketches of the ground about Quebec.

Shutting up his telescope, Wolfe sat silent a while. Then, as afterwards recorded by Robison, he turned towards his officers and repeated several stanzas of Gray's *Elegy*. 'Gentlemen,' he said as he ended, 'I would sooner have written that poem than beat the French tomorrow.' He did not know then that his own fame would far surpass the poet's, and that he should win it in the very way described in one of the lines he had just been quoting—

The paths of glory lead but to the grave.

At half-past eight in the evening he was sitting in his cabin on board Holmes's flagship, the *Sutherland*, above Cap Rouge, with 'Jacky

Jervis'—the future Earl St Vincent, but now the youngest captain in the fleet, only twenty-four. Wolfe and Jervis had both been at the same school at Greenwich, Swinden's, though at different times, and they were great friends. Wolfe had made up a sealed parcel of his notebook, his will, and the portrait of Katherine Lowther, and he now handed it over to Jervis for safe keeping.

But he had no chance of talking about old times at home, for just then a letter from the three brigadiers was handed in. It asked him if he would not give them 'distinct orders' about 'the place or places we are to attack.' He wrote back to the senior, Monckton, telling him what he had arranged for the first and second brigades, and then, separately, to Townshend about the third, which was not with Holmes but on the south shore. After dark the men from the island and the Point of Levy had marched up to join this brigade at Etchemin, the very place where Wolfe had made his plan on the 10th, as he stood and looked at the Foulon opposite.

His last general orders to his army had been read out some hours before; but, of course, the Foulon was not mentioned. These orders show that he well understood the great issues he was fighting for, and what men he had to count upon. Here are only three sentences; but how much they mean! 'The enemy's force is now divided. A vigorous blow struck by the army at this juncture may determine the fate of Canada. The officers and men will remember what their country expects of them.' The watchword was 'Coventry,' which, being probably suggested by the saying, 'Sent to Coventry,' that is, condemned to silence, was as apt a word for this expectant night as 'Gibraltar,' the symbol of strength, was for the one on which Quebec surrendered.

Just before dark Holmes sent every vessel he could spare to make a show of force opposite Pointe-aux-Trembles, in order to hold Bougainville there overnight. But after dark the main body of Holmes's squadron and all the boats and small transports came together opposite Cap Rouge. Just before ten a single lantern appeared in the *Sutherland's* main topmast shrouds. On seeing this, Chads formed up the boats between the ships and the south shore, the side away from the French. In three hours every man was in his place. Not a sound was to be heard except the murmur of the strong ebb-tide setting down towards Quebec and a gentle south-west breeze blowing in the same direction. 'All ready, sir!' and Wolfe took his own place in the first boat with his friend Captain Delaune, the leader of the twenty-four men of the 'Forlorn Hope,' who were to be the first to scale the cliff.

Then a second lantern appeared above the first; and the whole brigade of boats began to move off in succession. They had about eight miles to go. But the current ran the distance in two hours. As they advanced they could see the flashes from the Levis batteries growing brighter and more frequent; for both the land gunners there and the seamen gunners with Saunders farther down were increasing their fire as the hour for Wolfe's landing drew near.

A couple of miles above the Foulon the *Hunter* was anchored in midstream. As arranged, Chads left the south shore and steered straight for her. To his surprise he saw her crew training their guns on him. But they held their fire. Then Wolfe came alongside and found that she had two French deserters on board who had mistaken his boats for the French provision convoy that was expected to creep down the north shore that very night and land at the Foulon. He had already planned to pass his boats off as this convoy; for he knew that the farthest up of Holmes's men-of-war had stopped it above Pointe-aux-Trembles. But he was glad to know that the French posts below Cap Rouge had not yet heard of the stoppage.

From the *Hunter* his boat led the way to Sillery Point, half a mile above the Foulon. 'Halt! Who comes there!'—a French sentry's voice rang out in the silence of the night. 'France!' answered young Fraser, who had been taken into Wolfe's boat because he spoke French like a native. 'What's your regiment?' asked the sentry. 'The Queen's,' answered Fraser, who knew that this was the one supplying the escort for the provision boats the British had held up. 'But why don't you speak out?' asked the sentry again. 'Hush!' said Fraser, 'the British will hear us if you make a noise.' And there, sure enough, was the *Hunter*, drifting down, as arranged, not far outside the column of boats. Then the sentry let them all pass; and, in ten minutes more, exactly at four o'clock, the leading boat grounded in the Anse au Foulon and Wolfe jumped ashore.

He at once took the 'Forlorn Hope' and 200 light infantry to the side of the Cove towards Quebec, saying as he went, 'I don't know if we shall all get up, but we must make the attempt.' Then, while these men were scrambling up, he went back to the middle of the Cove, where Howe had already formed the remaining 500 light infantry. Captain Macdonald, a very active climber, passed the 'Forlorn Hope' and was the first man to reach the top and feel his way through the trees to the left, towards Vergor's tents. Presently he almost ran into the sleepy French-Canadian sentry, who heard only a voice speaking perfect French and telling him it was all right—nothing but the reinforcements from the Beauport camp; for Wolfe knew that Montcalm had been trying to get a French regular officer to replace Vergor, who was as good a thief as Bigot and as bad a soldier as Vaudreuil.

While this little parley was going on the 'Forlorn Hope' came up; when Macdonald promptly hit the sentry between the eyes with the hilt of his claymore and knocked him flat. The light infantry pressed on close behind. The dumbfounded French colonial troops coming out of their tents found themselves face to face with a whole woodful of fixed bayonets. They fired a few shots. The British charged with a loud cheer. The Canadians scurried away through the trees. And Vergor ran for dear life in his nightshirt.

The ringing cheer with which Delaune charged home told Wolfe at the foot of the road that the actual top was clear. Then Howe went up; and in fifteen minutes all the light infantry had joined their comrades above. Another battalion followed quickly, and Wolfe himself followed them. By this time it was five o'clock and quite light. The boats that had landed the first brigade had already rowed through the gaps between the small transports which were landing the second brigade, and had reached the south shore, a mile and a half away, where the third brigade was waiting for them.

Meanwhile the suddenly roused gunners of the Samos battery were firing wildly at the British vessels. But the men-of-war fired back with better aim, and Howe's light infantry, coming up at a run from behind, dashed in among the astonished gunners with the bayonet, cleared them all out, and spiked every gun. Howe left three companies there to hold the battery against Bougainville later in the day, and returned with the other seven to Wolfe. It was now six o'clock. The third brigade had landed, the whole of the ground at the top was clear; and Wolfe set off with 1,000 men to see what Montcalm was doing.

Quebec stands on the eastern end of a sort of promontory, or narrow tableland, between the St Lawrence and the valley of the St Charles. This tableland is less than a mile wide and narrows still more as it approaches Quebec. Its top is tilted over towards the St Charles and Beauport, the cliffs being only 100 feet high there, instead of 300, as they are beside the St Lawrence; so Wolfe, as he turned in towards Quebec, after marching straight across the tableland, could look out over the French camp. Everything seemed quiet; so he made his left secure and sent for his main body to follow him at once. It was now seven.

In another hour his line of battle was formed, his reserves had taken post in his rear, and a brigade of seamen from Saunders's fleet were landing guns, stores, blankets, tents, entrenching tools, and whatever else he would need for besieging the city after defeating Montcalm. The 3,000 sailors on the beach were anything but pleased with the tame work of waiting there while the soldiers were fighting up above. One of their officers, in a letter home, said they could hardly stand still, and were perpetually swearing because they were not allowed to get into the heat of action.

The whole of the complicated manoeuvres, in face of an active enemy, for three days and three nights, by land and water, over a front of thirty miles, had now been crowned by complete success. The army of 5,000 men had been put ashore at the right time and in the right way; and it was now ready to fight one of the great immortal battles of the world.

'*The thin red line.*' The phrase was invented long after Wolfe's day. But Wolfe invented the fact. The six battalions which formed his front, that thirteenth morning of September 1759, were drawn up in the first two-deep line that ever stood on any field of battle in the world since war began. And it was Wolfe alone who made this 'thin red line,' as surely as it was Wolfe alone who made the plan that conquered Canada.

Meanwhile Montcalm had not been idle; though he was perplexed to the last, because one of the stupid rules in the French camp was that all news was to be told first to Vaudreuil, who, as governor-general, could pass it on or not, and interfere with the army as much as he liked. When it was light enough to see Saunders's fleet, the island of Orleans, and the Point of Levy, Montcalm at once noticed that Wolfe's men had gone. He galloped down to the bridge of boats, where he found that Vaudreuil had already heard of Wolfe's landing. At first the French thought the firing round the Foulon was caused by an exchange of shots between the Samos battery and some British men-of-war that were trying to stop the French provision boats from getting in there. But Vergor's fugitives and the French patrols near Quebec soon told the real story. And then, just before seven, Montcalm himself caught sight of Wolfe's first redcoats marching in along the Ste Foy road. Well might he exclaim, after all he had done and Vaudreuil had undone: 'There they are, where they have no right to be!'

He at once sent orders, all along his six miles of entrenchments, to bring up every French regular and all the rest except 2,000 militia. But

Vaudreuil again interfered; and Montcalm got only the French and Canadian regulars, 2,500, and the same number of Canadian militia with a few Indians. The French and British totals, actually present on the field of battle, were, therefore, almost exactly equal, 5,000 each. Vaudreuil also forgot to order out the field guns, the horses for which the vile and corrupt Bigot had been using for himself. At nine Montcalm had formed up his French and colonial regulars between Quebec and the crest of rising ground across the Plains beyond which lay Wolfe.

Riding forward till he could see the redcoats, he noticed how thin their line was on its left and in its centre, and that its right, near the St Lawrence, had apparently not formed at all. But his eye deceived him about the British right, as the men were lying down there, out of sight, behind a swell of ground. He galloped back and asked if anyone had further news. Several officers declared they had heard that Wolfe was entrenching, but that his right brigade had not yet had time to march on to the field. There was no possible way of finding out anything else at once. The chance seemed favourable. Montcalm knew he had to fight or starve, as he was completely cut off by land and water, except for one bad, swampy road in the valley of the St Charles; and he ordered his line to advance.

At half-past nine the French reached the crest and halted. The two armies were now in full view of each other on the Plains and only a quarter of a mile apart. The French line of battle had eight small battalions, about 2,500 men, formed six deep. The colonial regulars, in three battalions, were on the flanks. The five battalions of French regulars were in the centre. Montcalm, wearing a green and gold uniform, with the brilliant cross of St Louis over his *cuirass*, and mounted on a splendid black charger, rode the whole length of his line, to see if all were ready to attack. The French regulars—half-fed, sorely harassed, interfered with by Vaudreuil—were still the victors of Ticonderoga, against the British odds of four to one. Perhaps they might snatch one last desperate victory from the fortunes of war? Certainly all would follow wherever they were led by their beloved Montcalm, the greatest Frenchman of the whole New World.

He said a few stirring words to each of his well-known regiments as he rode by; and when he laughingly asked the best of all, the Royal Roussillon, if they were not tired enough to take a little rest before the battle, they shouted back that they were never too tired to fight—'Forward, forward!' And their steady blue ranks, and those of the four white regiments beside them, with bayonets fixed and colours flying, did indeed look fit and ready for the fray.

Wolfe also had gone along his line of battle, the first of all two-deep thin red lines, to make sure that every officer understood the order that there was to be no firing until the French came close up, to within only forty paces. As soon as he saw Montcalm's line on the crest he had moved his own a hundred paces forward, according to previous arrangement; so that the two enemies were now only a long musket-shot apart. The Canadians and Indians were pressing round the British flanks, under cover of the bushes, and firing hard. But they were easily held in check by the light infantry on the left rear of the line and by the 35th on the right rear. The few French and British skirmishers in the centre now ran back to their own lines; and before ten the field was quite clear between the two opposing fronts.

Wolfe had been wounded twice when going along his line; first in the wrist and then in the groin. Yet he stood up so straight and looked so cool that when he came back to take post on the right the men there did not know he had been hit at all. His spirit already soared in triumph over the weakness of the flesh. Here he was, a sick and doubly wounded man; but a soldier, a hero, and a conqueror, with the key to half a continent almost within his eager grasp.

At a signal from Montcalm in the centre the French line advanced about a hundred yards in perfect formation. Then the Canadian regulars suddenly began firing without orders, and threw themselves flat on the ground to reload. By the time they had got up the French regulars had halted some distance in front of them, fired a volley, and begun advancing again. This was too much for the Canadians. Though they were regulars they were not used to fighting in the open, not trained for it, and not armed for it with bayonets. In a couple of minutes they had all slunk off to the flanks and joined the Indians and militia, who were attacking the British from under cover.

This left the French regulars face to face with Wolfe's front: five French battalions against the British six. These two fronts were now to decide the fate of Canada between them. The French still came bravely on; but their six-deep line was much shorter than the British two-deep line, and they saw that both their flanks were about to be over-lapped by fire and steel. They inclined outwards to save themselves from this fatal overlap on both right and left. But that made just as fatal a gap in their centre. Their whole line wavered, halted oftener to fire, and fired more wildly at each halt.

In the meantime Wolfe's front stood firm as a rock and silent as the grave, one long, straight, living wall of red, with the double line of deadly keen bayonets glittering above it. Nothing stirred along its whole length, except the Union Jacks, waving defiance at the *fleurs-de-lis*, and those patient men who fell before a fire to which they could not yet reply. Bayonet after bayonet would suddenly flash out of line and fall forward, as the stricken redcoat, standing there with shouldered arms, quivered and sank to the ground.

Captain York had brought up a single gun in time for the battle, the sailors having dragged it up the cliff and run it the whole way across the Plains. He had been handling it most gallantly during the French advance, firing showers of grape-shot into their ranks from a position right out in the open in front of Wolfe's line. But now that the French were closing he had to retire. The sailors then picked up the drag-ropes and romped in with this most effective six-pounder at full speed, as if they were having the greatest fun of their lives.

Wolfe was standing next to the Louisbourg Grenadiers, who, this time, were determined not to begin before they were told. He was to give their colonel the signal to fire the first volley; which then was itself to be the signal for a volley from each of the other five battalions, one after another, all down the line. Every musket was loaded with two bullets, and the moment a battalion had fired it was to advance twenty paces, loading as it went, and then fire a 'general,' that is, each man for himself, as hard as he could, till the bugles sounded the charge.

Wolfe now watched every step the French line made. Nearer and nearer it came. A hundred paces!—seventy-five!—fifty!—forty!!— *Fire!!!* Crash! came the volley from the grenadiers. Five volleys more rang out in quick succession, all so perfectly delivered that they sounded more like six great guns than six battalions with hundreds of muskets in each. Under cover of the smoke Wolfe's men advanced their twenty paces and halted to fire the 'general.' The dense, six-deep lines of Frenchmen reeled, staggered, and seemed to melt away under this awful deluge of lead. In five minutes their right was shaken out of all formation. All that remained of it turned and fled, a wild, mad mob of panic-stricken fugitives. The centre followed at once. But the Royal Roussillon stood fast a little longer; and when it also turned it had only three unwounded officers left, and they were trying to rally it.

Montcalm, who had led the centre and had been wounded in the advance, galloped over to the Royal Roussillon as it was making this last stand. But even he could not stem the rush that followed and that carried him along with it. Over the crest and down to the valley of the St Charles his army fled, the Canadians and Indians scurrying away through the bushes as hard as they could run. While making one more effort to rally enough men to cover the retreat he was struck again, this time by a dozen grape-shot from York's gun. He reeled in the saddle. But two of his grenadiers caught him and held him up while he rode into Quebec. As he passed through St Louis Gate a terrified woman called out, 'Oh! look at the *marquis*, he's killed, he's killed!' But Montcalm, by a supreme effort, sat up straight for a moment and said: 'It is nothing at all, my kind friend; you must not be so much alarmed!' and, saying this, passed on to die, a hero to the very last.

In the thick of the short, fierce fire-fight the bagpipes began to skirl, the Highlanders dashed down their muskets, drew their claymores, and gave a yell that might have been heard across the river. In a moment every British bugle was sounding the 'Charge' and the whole red, living wall was rushing forward with a roaring cheer.

But it charged without Wolfe. He had been mortally wounded just after giving the signal for those famous volleys. Two officers sprang to his side. 'Hold me up!' he implored them, 'don't let my gallant fellows see me fall!' With the help of a couple of men he was carried back to the far side of a little knoll and seated on a grenadier's folded coat, while the grenadier who had taken it off ran over to a spring to get some water. Wolfe knew at once that he was dying. But he did not yet know how the battle had gone. His head had sunk on his breast, and his eyes were already glazing, when an officer on the knoll called out, 'They run! They run! 'Egad, they give way everywhere!'

Rousing himself, as if from sleep, Wolfe asked, 'Who run?'

'The French, sir!'

'Then I die content!'—and, almost as he said it, he breathed his last.

He was not buried on the field he won, nor even in the country that he conquered. All that was mortal of him—his poor, sick, wounded body—was borne back across the sea, and carried in mourning triumph through his native land. And there, in the family vault at Greenwich, near the school he had left for his first war, half his short life ago, he was laid to rest on November 20—at the very time when his own great victory before Quebec was being confirmed by Hawke's magnificently daring attack on the French fleet amid all the dangers of that wild night in Quiberon Bay.

Canada has none of his mortality. But could she have anything more sacred than the spot from which his soaring spirit took its flight into immortal fame? And could this sacred spot be marked by any words more winged than these:

HERE DIED
WOLFE
VICTORIOUS

CHAPTER 8

Epilogue—The Last Stand

Wolfe's victory on the Plains of Abraham proved decisive in the end; but it was not the last of the great struggle for the Key of Canada.

After Wolfe had died on the field of battle, and Monckton had been disabled by his wounds, Townshend took command, received the surrender of Quebec on the 18th, and waited till the French field army had retired towards Montreal. Then he sailed home with Saunders, leaving Murray to hold what Wolfe had won. Saunders left Lord Colville in charge of a strong squadron, with orders to wait at Halifax till the spring.

Both French and British spent a terrible winter. The French had better shelter in Montreal than the British had among the ruins of Quebec; and, being more accustomed to the rigours of the climate, they would have suffered less from cold in any case. But their lot was, on the whole, the harder of the two; for food was particularly bad and scarce in Montreal, where even horseflesh was thought a luxury. Both armies were ravaged by disease to a most alarming extent. Of the eight thousand men with whom Murray began that deadly winter not one-half were able to bear arms in the spring; and not one-half of those who did bear arms then were really fit for duty.

Montcalm's successor, Levis, now made a skilful, bold, and gallant attempt to retake Quebec before navigation opened. Calling the whole remaining strength of New France to his aid, he took his army down in April, mostly by way of the St Lawrence. The weather was stormy. The banks of the river were lined with rotting ice. The roads were almost impassable. Yet, after a journey of less than ten days, the whole French army appeared before Quebec. Murray was at once confronted by a dire dilemma. The landward defences had never been strong; and he had not been able to do more than patch them up.

If he remained behind them Levis would close in, batter them down, and probably carry them by assault against a sickly garrison depressed by being kept within the walls. If, on the other hand, he marched out, he would have to meet more than double numbers at the least; for some men would have to be left to cover a retreat; and he knew the French grand total was nearly thrice his own. But he chose this bolder course; and at the chill dawn of April 28, he paraded his little attacking force of a bare three thousand men on the freezing snow and mud of the Esplanade and then marched out.

The two armies met at Ste Foy, a mile and a half beyond the walls; and a desperate battle ensued. The French had twice as many men in action, but only half of these were regulars; the others had no bayonets; and there was no effective artillery to keep down the fire of Murray's commanding guns. The terrific fight went on for hours, while victory inclined neither to one side nor the other. It was a far more stubborn and much bloodier contest than Wolfe's of the year before. At last a British battalion was fairly caught in flank by overwhelming numbers and driven across the front of Murray's guns, whose protecting fire it thus completely masked at a most critical time. Murray thereupon ordered up his last reserve. But even so he could no longer stand his ground. Slowly and sullenly his exhausted men fell back before the French, who put the very last ounce of their own failing strength into a charge that took the guns. Then the beaten British staggered in behind their walls, while the victorious French stood fast, worn out by the hardships of their march and fought to a standstill in the battle.

Levis rallied his army for one more effort and pressed the siege to the uttermost of his power. Murray had lost a thousand men and could now muster less than three thousand. Each side prepared to fight the other to the death. But both knew that the result would depend on the fleets. There had been no news from Europe since navigation closed; and hopes ran high among the besiegers that perhaps some friendly men-of-war might still be first; when of course Quebec would have to surrender at discretion, and Canada would certainly be saved for France if the half-expected peace would only follow soon.

Day after day all eyes, both French and British, looked seaward from the heights and walls; though fleets had never yet been known to come up the St Lawrence so early in the season. At last, on May 9, the tops of a man-of-war were sighted just beyond the Point of Levy. Either she or Quebec, or both, might have false colours flying.

So neither besiegers nor besieged knew to which side she belonged. Nor did she know herself whether Quebec was French or British. Slowly she rounded into the harbour, her crew at quarters, her decks all cleared for action. She saluted with twenty-one guns and swung out her captain's barge. Then, for the first time, every one watching knew what she was; for the barge was heading straight in towards the town, and redcoats and bluejackets could see each other plainly. In a moment every British soldier who could stand had climbed the nearest wall and was cheering her to the echo; while the gunners showed their delight by loading and firing as fast as possible and making all the noise they could.

But one ship was not enough to turn the scale; and Levis redoubled his efforts. On the night of the 15th French hopes suddenly flared up all through the camp when the word flew round that three strange men-of-war just reported down off Beauport were the vanguard of a great French fleet. But daylight showed them to be British, and British bent on immediate and vigorous attack. Two of these frigates made straight for the French flotilla, which fled in wild confusion, covered by the undaunted Vauquelin in the *Atalante*, which fought a gallant rearguard action all the twenty miles to Pointe-aux-Trembles, where she was driven ashore and forced to strike her colours, after another, and still more desperate, resistance of over two hours. That night Levis raised the siege in despair and retired on Montreal. Next morning Lord Colville arrived with the main body of the fleet, having made the earliest ascent of the St Lawrence ever known to naval history, before that time or since.

Then came the final scene of all this moving drama. Step by step overpowering British forces closed in on the doomed and dwindling army of New France. They closed in from east and west and south, each one of their converging columns more than a match for all that was left of the French. Whichever way he looked, Levis could see no loophole of escape. There was nothing but certain defeat in front and on both flanks, and starvation in the rear. So when the advancing British met, all together, at the island of Montreal, he and his faithful regulars laid down their arms without dishonour, in the fully justifiable belief that no further use of them could possibly retrieve the great lost cause of France in Canada.

The Passing of New France: a Chronicle of
Montcalm

Montcalm at the Battle of the Plains, 1759

Contents

CHAPTER 1

Montcalm in France 1712–1756

'*War is the grave of the Montcalms.*' No one can tell how old this famous saying is. Perhaps it is as old as France herself. Certainly there never was a time when the men of the great family of Montcalm-Gozon were not ready to fight for their king and country; and so Montcalm, like Wolfe, was a soldier born.

Even in the Crusades his ancestors were famous all over Europe. When the Christians of those brave days were trying to drive the unbelievers out of Palestine they gladly followed leaders whom they thought saintly and heroic enough to be their champions against the dragons of *sultan*, Satan, and hell; for people then believed that dragons fought on the devil's side, and that only Christian knights, like St George, fighting on God's side, could kill them. The Christians banded themselves together in many ways, among others in the Order of the Knights of St John of Jerusalem, taking an oath to be faithful unto death. They chose the best man among them to be their Grand Master; and so it could have been only after much devoted service that Deodat de Gozon became Grand Master, more than five hundred years ago, and was granted the right of bearing the conquered Dragon of Rhodes on the family coat of arms, where it is still to be seen. How often this glorious badge of victory reminded our own Montcalm of noble deeds and noble men! How often it nerved him to uphold the family tradition!

There are centuries of change between Crusaders and Canadians. Yet the Montcalms can bridge them with their honour. And, among all the Montcalms who made their name mean soldier's honour in Eastern or European war, none have given it so high a place in the world's history as the hero whose life and death in Canada made it immortal. He won the supreme glory for his name, a glory so bright that it shone even through the dust of death which shrouded the France of the Revolution. In 1790, when the National Assembly was suppressing pensions granted by the Crown, it made a special exception in favour of Montcalm's children. As kings, *marquises*, heirs, and pensions were among the things the Revolution hated most, it is a notable tribute to our Marquis of Montcalm that the revolutionary parliament should have paid to his heirs the pension granted by a king. Nor has another century of change in France blotted out his name and fame.

The *Montcalm* was the French flagship at the naval review held in honour of the coronation of King Edward VII. The *Montcalm* took the President of France to greet his ally the Czar of Russia. And, but for a call of duty elsewhere at the time, the *Montcalm* would have flown the French admiral's flag in 1908, at the celebration of the Tercentenary of the founding of Quebec, when King George V led the French- and English-speaking peoples of the world in doing honour to the twin renown of Wolfe and Montcalm on the field where they won equal glory, though unequal fortune.

Montcalm was a leapyear baby, having been born on February 29, 1712, in the family castle of Candiac, near Nimes, a very old city of the south of France, a city with many forts built by the Romans two thousand years ago. He came by almost as much good soldier blood on his mother's side as on his father's, for she was one of the Castellanes, with numbers of heroic ancestors, extending back to the First Crusade.

The Montcalms had never been rich. They had many heroes but no millionaires. Yet they were well known and well loved for their kindness to all the people on their estates; and so generous to everyone in trouble, and so ready to spend their money as well as their lives for the sake of king and country, that they never could have made great fortunes, even had their estate been ten times as large as it was. Accordingly, while they were famous and honoured all over France, they had to be very careful about spending money on themselves. They all—and our own Montcalm in particular—spent much more in serving their country than their country ever spent in paying them to serve it.

Montcalm was a delicate little boy of six when he first went to school. He had many schoolboy faults. He found it hard to keep quiet or to pay attention to his teacher; he was backward in French grammar; and he wrote a very bad hand. Many a letter of complaint was sent to his father. 'It seems to me,' writes the teacher, 'that his hand-writing is getting worse than ever. I show him, again and again, how to hold his pen; but he will not do it properly. I think he ought to try to make up for his want of cleverness by being more docile, taking more pains, and listening to my advice.' And then poor old Dumas would end with an exclamation of despair—'What will become of him!'

Dumas had another pupil who was much more to his taste. This was Montcalm's younger brother, Jean, who knew his letters before he was three, read Latin when he was five, and Greek and Hebrew when he was six. Dumas was so proud of this infant prodigy that he took him to Paris and showed him off to the learned men of the day, who were dumbfounded at so much knowledge in so young a boy. All this, however, was too much for a youthful brain; and poor Jean died at the age of seven.

Dumas then turned sadly to the elder boy, who was in no danger of being killed by too much study, and soon renewed his complaints. At last Montcalm, now sixteen and already an officer, could bear it no longer, and wrote to his father telling him that in spite of his supposed stupidity he had serious aims.

I want to be, first, a man of honour, brave, and a good Christian. Secondly, I want to read moderately; to know as much Greek and Latin as other men; also arithmetic, history, geography, lit-erature, and some art and science. Thirdly, I want to be obedient to you and my dear mother; and listen to Mr Dumas's advice. Lastly, I want to manage a horse and handle a sword as well as ever I can.

The result of it all was that Montcalm became a good Latin scholar, a very well read man, an excellent horseman and swordsman, and—to dominie Dumas's eternal confusion—such a master of French that he might have been as great an author as he was a soldier. His letters and dispatches from the seat of war remind one of Caesar's. He wrote like a man who sees into the heart of things and goes straight to the point with the fewest words which will express exactly what he wishes to say. In this he was like Wolfe, and like many another great soldier whose quick eye, cool head and warm heart, all working together in the service of his country, give him a command over words which often equals his command over men.

In 1727, the year Wolfe was born, Montcalm joined his father's regiment as an ensign. Presently, in 1733, the French and Germans fell out over the naming of a king for Poland. Montcalm went to the front and had what French soldiers call his 'baptism of fire.' This war gave him little chance of learning how great battles should be fought. But he saw two sieges; he kept his eyes open to everything that happened; and, even in camp, he did not forget his studies. 'I am learning German,' he wrote home, 'and I am reading more Greek than I have read for three or four years.'

The death of his father in 1735 made him the head of the family of Montcalm. The next year he married Angelique Talon du Boulay, a member of a military family, and grand-daughter of Denis Talon; a kinsman of Jean Talon, the best *intendant* who ever served New France. For the next twenty years, from 1736 to 1756, he spent in his ancestral castle of Candiac as much of his time as he could spare from the army. There he had been born, and there he always hoped he could live and die among his own people after his wars were over. How often he was to sigh for one look at his pleasant olive groves when he was far away, upholding the honour of France against great British odds and, far worse, against secret enemies on the French side in the dying colony across the sea! But for the present all this was far off. Meanwhile, Candiac was a very happy home; and Montcalm's wife and his mother made it the happier by living together under the same roof. In course of time ten children were born, all in the family *chateau*.

Montcalm's second war was the War of the Austrian Succession, a war in which his younger opponent Wolfe saw active service for the first time. The two future opponents in Canada never met, however, on the same battlefields in Europe. In 1741, the year in which Wolfe received his first commission, Montcalm fought so well in Bohemia that he was made a Knight of St Louis. Two years later, at the age of thirty-one, he was promoted to the command of a regiment which he led through three severe campaigns in Italy. During the third campaign, in 1746, there was a terrific fight against the Austrians under the walls of Placentia. So furious was the Austrian attack that the French army was almost destroyed. Twice was Montcalm's regiment broken by sheer weight of numbers. But twice he rallied it and turned to face the enemy again.

The third attack was the worst of all. Montcalm still fought on, though already he had three bullet wounds, when the Austrian cavalry made a dashing charge and swept the French off the field altogether. He met them, sword in hand, as dauntless as ever; but he was caught in a whirlwind of sabre-cuts and was felled to the ground with two great gashes in his head. He was taken prisoner; but was soon allowed to go home, on giving his word of honour, or 'parole,' that he would take no further part in the war until some Austrian prisoner, of the same rank as his own, was given back by the French in exchange. While still on parole he was promoted to be a brigadier, so that he could command more than a single regiment. In due time, when proper exchange of prisoners was made, Montcalm went back to Italy, again fought splendidly, and again was badly wounded. The year 1748 closed with the Treaty of Aix-la-Chapelle; and seven years of peace followed before the renewed tumult of the Seven Years' War.

Life went very well with Montcalm at Candiac. He was there as much as possible, and spent his time between his castle and his olive groves, his study and his family circle. His eldest son was a young man of much promise, growing immensely tall, devoted to the army, and engaged to be married. His wife and her mother-in-law were as happy as ever with him and with each other. Nothing seemed more peaceful than that quiet corner in the pleasant land of southern France.

But the age-long rivalry of French and British could not long be stilled. Even in 1754 there were rumours of war from the Far East in India and from the Far West in Canada. Next year, though peace was outwardly kept in Europe, both the great rivals sent fleets and armies to America, where the clash of arms had already been heard. There were losses on both sides. And, when the French general, Baron Dieskau, was made prisoner, the Minister of War, knowing the worth of Montcalm, asked him to think over the proposal that he should take command in New France.

On January 26, 1756, the formal offer came in a letter approved by the king.

The king has chosen you to command his troops in North America, and will honour you on your departure with the rank of major-general. But what will please you still more is that His Majesty will put your son in your place at the head of your present regiment. The applause of the public will add to your satisfaction.

On the very day Montcalm received this letter he made up his mind, accepted the command, bade goodbye to Candiac, and set out for Paris. From Lyons he wrote to his mother:

I am reading with much pleasure the History of New France by Father Charlevoix. He gives a pleasant description of Quebec.

Montcalm

From Paris he wrote to his wife:

'Do not expect any long letter before the 1st of March. All my pressing work will then be finished, and I shall be able to breathe once more. Last night I came from Versailles and I am going back tomorrow. My outfit will cost me a thousand crowns more than the amount I am paid to cover it. But I cannot stop for that.' On March 15 he wrote home: 'Yesterday I presented my son, with whom I am very well pleased, to all the royal family.' Three days later he wrote to his wife: 'I shall be at Brest on the twenty-first. My son has been here since yesterday, for me to coach him and also in order to get his uniform properly made. He will thank the king for his promotion at the same time that I make my *adieux* in my embroidered coat. Perhaps I shall leave some debts behind me. I wait impatiently for the accounts. You have my will. I wish you would have it copied, and would send me the duplicate before I sail.'

On April 3 Montcalm left Brest in the *Licorne*, a ship of the little fleet which the French were hurrying out to Canada before war should be declared in Europe. The passage proved long and stormy. But Montcalm was lucky in being a much better sailor than his great opponent Wolfe. Impatient to reach the capital at the earliest possible moment he rowed ashore from below the island of Orleans, where the *Licorne* met a contrary wind, and drove up to Quebec, a distance of twenty-five miles. It was May 13 when he first passed along the Beauport shore between Montmorency and Quebec. Three years and nine days later he was to come back to that very point, there to make his last heroic stand. On the evening of his arrival Bigot the *intendant* gave a magnificent dinner-party for him. Forty guests sat down to the banquet. Montcalm had not expected that the poor struggling colony could boast such a scene as this. In a letter home he said:

> Even a Parisian would have been astonished at the profusion of good things on the table. Such splendour and good cheer show how much the *intendant's* place is worth.

We shall soon hear more of Bigot the *intendant*.

On the 26th Montcalm arrived at Montreal to see the Marquis of Vaudreuil the governor. The meeting went off very well. The governor was as full of airs and graces as the *intendant*, and said that nothing else in the world could have given him so much pleasure as to greet the general sent out to take command of the troops from France. We shall soon hear more of Vaudreuil the governor.

CHAPTER 2

Montcalm in Canada 1756

The French colonies in North America consisted of nothing more than two very long and very thin lines of scattered posts and settlements, running up the St Lawrence and the Mississippi to meet, in the far interior, at the Great Lakes. Along the whole of these four thousand miles there were not one hundred thousand people. Only two parts of the country were really settled at all: one Acadia, the other the shores of the St Lawrence between Bic and Montreal; and both regions together covered not more than four hundred of the whole four thousand miles. There were but three considerable towns—Louisbourg, Quebec, and Montreal—and Quebec, which was much the largest, had only twelve thousand inhabitants.

The territory bordering on the Mississippi was called Louisiana. That in the St Lawrence region was called New France along the river and Acadia down by the Gulf; though Canada is much the best word to cover both. Now, Canada had ten times as many people as Louisiana; and Louisiana by itself seemed helplessly weak. This very weakness made the French particularly anxious about the country south of the Lakes, where Canada and Louisiana met. For, so long as they held it, they held the gateways of the West, kept the valleys of the Ohio and Mississippi quite securely, shut up the British colonies between the Alleghany Mountains and the Atlantic and prevented them from expanding westward. One other thing was even more vital than this to the French in America: it was that they should continue to hold the mouth of the St Lawrence. Canada could live only by getting help from France; and as this help could not come up the Mississippi it had to come up the St Lawrence.

The general position of the French may be summed up briefly. First, and most important of all, they had to hold the line of the St

PACIFIC OCEAN

Hudson
Bay

RUPERT'S LAND
THE HUDSONS BAY CO.

Cape B
Saskatchewan
L.Winnipeg
Albany

L. of
The Woods

CANADA OR NEW FRANCE

Montreal
Quebec
Thousand Islands
Albany
Boston

ENGLISH COLONIES

Ft.Duquesne
Vincennes
Ohio R.
Kaskaskia
Arkansas R.
LOUISIANA
Red R.

New York
Philadelphia
Wilmington
St.Mary's

ATLANTIC OCEAN

St.John's
Cape Breton I.
Louisbourg
Halifax
Plymouth
Providence

Newfoundland

Annapolis

Santa Fe
Gila R.
NEW
Rio Grande
Pensacola
New Orleans

Wilmington
Charleston
Port Royal
St.Augustine

Bermudas

GULF OF
MEXICO

Havana
CUBA
Mexico
BELIZE
GUATEMALA
Jamaica
Bahama Is.
Hayti
San Domingo
Porto
Rico
I. OF HAYTI
CARIBBEAN SEA

SOUTH
AMERICA

NORTH AMERICA
1755 - 80
English Miles
0   100 200 300 400 500   700
English
French
Spanish
Unexplored

Lawrence for a thousand miles in from the sea. Here were their three chief positions: Louisbourg, Quebec, and Lake Champlain.

Secondly, they had to hold another thousand miles westward, to and across the Lakes; but especially the country south of Lakes Ontario and Erie, into the valley of the Ohio. Here there were a few forts, but no settlements worth speaking of.

Thirdly, they had to hold the valley of the Mississippi, two thousand miles from north to south. Here there were very few forts, very few men, and no settlements of any kind. In fact, they held the Mississippi only by the merest thread, and chiefly because the British colonies had not yet grown out in that direction. The Mississippi did not come into the war, though it might have done so. If Montcalm had survived the battle of the Plains, and if in 1760 the defence of Canada on the St Lawrence had seemed to him utterly hopeless, his plan would probably then have been to take his best soldiers from Canada into the interior, and in the end to New Orleans, there to make a last desperate stand for France among the swamps. But this plan died with him; and we may leave the valley of the Mississippi out of our reckoning altogether.

Not so the valley of the Ohio, which, as we have seen, was the meeting-place of Canada and Louisiana, and the chief gateway to the West; and which the French and British rivals were both most fiercely set on possessing. It was here that the worldwide Seven Years' War first broke out; here that George Washington first appeared as an American commander; here that Braddock led the first westbound British army; and here that Montcalm struck his first blow for French America.

But, as we have also seen, even the valley of the Ohio was less important than the line of the St Lawrence. The Ohio region was certainly the right arm of French America. But the St Lawrence was the body, of which the lungs were Louisbourg, and the head and heart Quebec. Montcalm saw this at once; and he made no single mistake in choosing the proper kind of attack and defence during the whole of his four campaigns.

The British colonies were different in every way from the French. The French held a long, thin line of four thousand miles, forming an inland loop from the Gulf of St Lawrence to the Gulf of Mexico, with only one hundred thousand people sparsely settled in certain spots; the British filled up the solid inside of this loop with over twelve hundred thousand people, who had an open seaboard on the Atlantic for two thousand miles, from Nova Scotia down to Florida.

Now, what could have made such a great difference in growth between the French and the British colonies, when France had begun with all the odds of European force and numbers in her favour? The answer is two-fold: France had no adequate fleets and her colonies had no adequate freedom.

First, as to fleets. The mere fact that the Old and New Worlds had a sea between them meant that the power with the best navy would have a great advantage. The Portuguese, Spaniards, Dutch, and French all tried to build empires across the sea. But they all failed whenever they came to blows with Britain, simply because no empire can live cut up into separate parts. The sea divided the other empires, while, strange as it may appear, this same sea united the British. The French were a nation of landsmen; for one very good reason that they had two land frontiers to defend. Their kings and statesmen understood armies better than navies, and the French people themselves liked soldiers better than sailors. The British, on the other hand, since they lived on an island, had no land frontiers to defend. The people liked sailors better than soldiers. And their rulers understood navies better than armies, for the sea had always been the people's second home.

At this period, whenever war broke out, the British navy was soon able to win 'the command of the sea'; that is, its squadrons soon made the sea a safe road for British ships and a very unsafe road for the ships of an enemy. In America, at that time, everything used in war, from the regular fleets and armies themselves down to the powder and shot, cannon and muskets, swords and bayonets, tools, tents, and so on—all had to be brought across the Atlantic. While this was well enough for the British, for the French it was always very hard and risky work. In time of war their ships were watched, chased and taken whenever they appeared on the sea. Even during peace they had much the worse of it, for they had to spend great sums and much effort in building vessels to make up for the men of-war and the merchant ships which they had lost and the British had won. Thus they never quite succeeded in beginning again on even terms with their triumphant rival.

We must remember, too, that every sort of trade and money-making depended on the command of the sea, which itself depended on the stronger navy. Even the trade with Indians in America, two thousand miles inland, depended on defeat or victory at sea. The French might send out ships full of things to exchange for valuable furs. But if they lost their ships they lost their goods, and in consequence the trade and even the friendship of the Indians. In the same way the navy helped or hindered the return trade from America to Europe. The furs and food from the British colonies crossed over in safety, and the money or other goods in exchange came safely back. But the French ships were not safe, and French merchants were often ruined by the capture of their ships or by having the sea closed to them.

To follow out all the causes and effects of the command of the sea would be far too long a story even to begin here. But the gist of it is quite short and quite plain: no navy, no Empire. That is what it meant then, and that is what it means now.

Secondly, as to freedom in the French colonies. Of course, freedom itself, no matter how good it is and how much we love it, would have been nothing without the protection of fleets. All the freedom in the world cannot hold two countries on opposite sides of the sea together without the link of strong fleets. But even the strongest fleet would not have helped New France to grow as fast and as well as New England grew. The French people were not free in the motherland. They were not free as colonists in Canada. All kinds of laws and rules were made for the Canadians by persons thousands of miles away. This interference came from men who knew scarcely anything about Canada. They had crude notions as to what should be done, and sometimes they ordered the men on the spot to do impossible things. The result was that the men on the spot, if they were bad enough and clever enough, just hoodwinked the government in France, and did in Canada what they liked and what made for their own profit.

Now, Bigot the *intendant*, the man of affairs in the colony, was on the spot; and he was one of the cleverest knaves ever known, with a feeble colony in his power. He had nothing to fear from the people, the poor, helpless French Canadians. He had nothing to fear from their governor, the vain, incompetent Vaudreuil. He was, moreover, three thousand miles away from the French court, which was itself full of parasites. He had been given great power in Canada. As *intendant* he was the head of everything except the army, the navy, and the church. He had charge of all the public money and all the public works and whatever else might be called public business. Of course, he was supposed to look after the interests of France and of Canada, not after his own; and earlier *intendants* like Talon had done this with perfect honesty. But Bigot soon organized a gang of men like himself, and gathered into his grasping hands the control of the private as well as of the public business.

One example will show how he worked. Whenever food became

dangerously scarce in Canada the *intendant's* duty was to buy it up, to put it into the king's stores, and to sell out only enough for the people to live on till the danger was over. There was a reason for this, as Canada, cut off from France, was like a besieged fortress, and it was proper to treat the people as a garrison would be treated, and to make provision for the good of the whole. But when Bigot had formed his gang, and had, in some way, silenced Vaudreuil, he declared Canada in danger when it was not, seized all the food he could lay hands on, and sent it over to France; sent it, too, in the king's ships, that it might be carried free. Then he made Vaudreuil send word to the king that Canada was starving.

In the meantime, his friends in France had stored the food, and had then assured the king that there was plenty of grain in hand which they could ship to Canada at once. The next step was to get an order from the king to buy this food to be shipped to Canada. This order was secured through influential friends in Paris, and, of course, the price paid by the king was high. The food was then sent back to Canada, again in the king's ships. Then Bigot and his friends in Canada put it not into the king's but into their own stores in Quebec, sold it to the king's stores once more, as they had sold it in France, and then effected a third sale, this time to the wretched French Canadians from whom they had bought it for next to nothing at first. Thus both the king and the French Canadians were each robbed twice over, thanks to Vaudreuil's complaisance and Bigot's official position as also representing the king.

Bigot had been some time in Canada before Vaudreuil arrived as governor in 1755. He had already cheated a good deal. But it was only when he found out what sort of man Vaudreuil was that he set to work to do his worst. Bigot was a knave, Vaudreuil a fool. Vaudreuil was a French Canadian born and very jealous of any one from France, unless the Frenchman flattered him as Bigot did. He loved all sorts of pomp and show, and thought himself the greatest man in America. Bigot played on this weakness with ease and could persuade him to sign any orders, no matter how bad they were.

Now, when an owl like Vaudreuil and a fox like Bigot were ruining Canada between them, they were anything but pleased to see a lion like Montcalm come out with an army from France. Vaudreuil, indeed, had done all he could to prevent the sending out of Montcalm. He wrote to France several times, saying that no French general was needed, that separate regiments under their own colonels would suffice, and that he himself could command the regulars from France, just as he did the Canadians.

But how did he command the Canadians? By law every Canadian had to serve as a soldier, without pay, whenever the country was in danger. By law every man needed for carrying supplies to the far-off outposts could also be taken; but, in this case, he had to be paid. Now, all the supplies and the carriage of them were under Bigot's care. So when the Canadians were called out as soldiers, without pay, Bigot's gang would ask them if they would rather go and be shot for nothing or carry supplies in safety for pay. Of course, they chose the carrier's work and the pay, though half the pay was stolen from them. At the same time their names were still kept on the muster rolls as soldiers. This was the reason why Montcalm often had only half the militia called out for him: the other half were absent as carriers, and the half which remained for Montcalm was made up of those men whom Bigot's friends did not think good enough for carriers.

But there were more troubles still for Montcalm and his army. As governor, Vaudreuil was, of course, the head of everything in the country, including the army. This was right enough, if he had been fit for his post, because a country must have a supreme head, and the army is only a part, though the most important part, in war. A soldier may be also a statesman and at the head of everything, as were Cromwell, Napoleon, and Frederick the Great. But a statesman who is not a soldier only ruins an army if he tries to command it himself. And this was precisely what Vaudreuil did. Indeed, he did worse, for, while he did not go into the field himself, he continued to give orders to Montcalm at every turn. Besides, instead of making all the various forces on the French side into one army he kept them as separate as he could—five parts and no whole.

It should be made clear what these five parts were. First, there were the French regulars, the best of all, commanded by Montcalm, who was himself under Vaudreuil. Next, there were the Canadian regulars and the Canadian militia, both directly under Vaudreuil. Then there were the French sailors, under their own officers, but subject to Vaudreuil. Montcalm had to report to the Minister of War in Paris about the French regulars, and to the Minister of Marine about the Canadians of both kinds. Vaudreuil reported to both ministers, usually against Montcalm; and the French naval commander reported to his own minister on his own account. So there was abundant opportunity to make trouble among the four French forces. But there was more

VAUDREUIL

trouble still with the fifth force, the Indians, who were under their own chiefs. These men admired Montcalm; but they had to make treaties with Vaudreuil. They were cheated by Bigot and were offered presents by the British. As they very naturally desired to keep their own country for themselves in their own way they always wished to side with the stronger of the two white rivals, if they could not get rid of both.

Such was the Canada of 1756, a country in quite as much danger from French parasites as from British patriots. It might have lasted for some years longer if there had been no general war. The American colonists, though more than twelve to one, could not have conquered it alone, because they had no fleet and no regular army. But the war came, and it was a great one. In a great war a country of parasites has no chance against a country of patriots. All the sins of sloth and wilful weakness, of demagogues and courtiers, and whatever else is rotten in the state, are soon found out and punished by war. Canada under Vaudreuil and Bigot was no match for an empire under Pitt. For one's own parasites are always the worst of one's enemies. So the last great fight for Canada was not a fight of three against three; but of one against five. Montcalm the lion stood utterly alone, with two secret foes behind him and three open foes in front—Vaudreuil the owl, and Bigot the fox, behind; Pitt, Saunders and Wolfe, three lions like himself, in front.

CHAPTER 3

Oswego 1756

In 1753 the governor of Virginia had sent Washington, then a young major of only twenty-one, to see what the French were doing in the valley of the Ohio, where they had been busy building forts to shut the gateway of the West against the British and to keep it open for themselves. The French officers at a post which they called Venango received Washington very politely and asked him to supper. Washington wrote in his diary that, after they had drunk a good deal of wine, 'they told me that it was their absolute design to take possession of the Ohio, and by God they would do it.' When Washington had returned home and reported, the Virginians soon sent him back with a small force to turn the French out. But meanwhile the French had been making themselves much stronger, and on July 4, 1754, when Washington advanced into the disputed territory, he was overcome and obliged to surrender—a strange Fourth of July for him to look back upon!

Exciting events followed rapidly. In 1755 Braddock came out from England with a small army of regulars to take command of the British forces in America and drive the French from the Ohio valley. But there were many difficulties. The governments of the thirteen British colonies were jealous of each other and of the government in Britain; their militia were jealous of the British regulars, who in turn looked down on them. In the end, with only a few Virginians to assist him, Braddock marched into a country perfectly new to him and his men. The French and Indians, quite at home in the dense forest, laid an ambush for the British regulars. These stood bravely, but they could not see a single enemy to fire at. They were badly defeated, and Braddock was killed.

The British had a compensating success a few weeks later when, in the centre of Canada, beside Lake George, the French general, Baron Dieskau, was defeated almost as badly as Braddock had been. Following this, down by the Gulf the French Acadians were rooted out of Nova Scotia, for fear that they might join the other French in the coming war. Their lot was a hard one, but as they had been British subjects for forty years and had always refused to take the oath of allegiance to the British crown, and as they were being constantly stirred up against British rule, it was decided that they could not be safely left inside the British frontier.

At sea the French had also suffered loss. Admiral Boscawen had seized two ships with four hundred seasoned French regulars on board destined for Canada. The French then sent out another four hundred to replace them. But no veteran soldiers could be spared. So the second four hundred, raised from all sorts of men, were of poor quality, and spoiled the discipline of the regiments they joined in Canada. One of the regiments, which had the worst of these recruits, proved to be the least trust. worthy in the final struggle before Quebec in 1759. Thus the power of the British navy in the Gulf of St Lawrence in 1755 made itself felt four years later, and a long distance away, at the very crisis of the war on land.

Strange as it seems to us now, all this fighting had taken place in a time of nominal peace. But in 1756 the Seven Years' War broke out in Europe, and then many plans were made, especially in the English colonies in America, for the conquest of Canada. The British forces were greater than the French, all told on both sides, both then and throughout the war. But the thirteen colonies could not agree. Some of them were hot, others lukewarm, others, such as the Quakers of Pennsylvania, cold. Moreover, the British generals were of little use, and the colonial ones squabbled as the colonies themselves squabbled. Pitt had not yet taken charge of the war, and the British in America were either doing nothing or doing harm.

There was only one trained and competent general on the whole continent; and that general was Montcalm. Though new to warfare in the wilds he soon understood it as well as those who had waged it all their lives; and he saw at a glance that an attack on Oswego was the key to the whole campaign. Louisbourg was, as yet, safe enough; and the British movements against Lake Champlain were so slow and foolish that he turned them to good account for his own purposes.

At the end of June, 1756, Montcalm arrived at Ticonderoga, where he had already posted his second-in-command, the Chevalier de Levis, with 3,000 men. He walked all over the country thereabouts and seized the lie of the land so well that he knew it thoroughly when he came back, two years later, and won his greatest victory. He kept his men busy too. He moved them forward so boldly and so cleverly that the British who had been planning the capture of the fort never thought of attacking him, but made sure only of defending themselves. All this was but a feint to put the British off their guard elsewhere. Suddenly, while Levis kept up the show of force, Montcalm himself left secretly for Montreal, saw Vaudreuil, who, like Bigot, was still all bows and smiles, and left again, with equal suddenness, for Fort Frontenac (now Kingston) on July 21. From this point he intended to attack Oswego.

At the entrance to the Thousand Islands there was a point, called by the voyageurs Point Baptism, where every new-comer into the 'Upper Countries' had to pay the old hands to drink his health. The French regulars, 1,300 strong, were all new to the West, and, as they formed nearly half of Montcalm's little army, the 'baptism' of so many newcomers caused a great deal of jollity in camp that night. Serious work was, however, ahead. Fort Frontenac was reached on the 29th; and here the report that Villiers, with the advance guard, had already taken from the British 200 canoes and 300 prisoners soon flew round and raised the men's spirits to the highest pitch.

Montcalm at once sent out two armed ships, with twenty-eight cannon between them, to cut off Oswego by water, while he sent a picked body of Canadians and Indians into the woods on the south shore to cut the place off by land. There was no time to lose, since the British were, on the whole, much stronger, and might make up their slow minds to send an army to the rescue. Montcalm lost not a moment. He sailed across the lake with his 3,000 men and all his guns and stores, and landed at Sackett's Harbour, which his advance guard had already seized and prepared. Then, hiding in the mouths of rivers by day and marching and rowing by night, his army arrived safely within cannon-shot of Oswego under cover of the dark on August 10.

There were three forts at the mouth of the Oswego. The first was Fort Ontario; then, across the river, stood Fort Oswego; and, beyond that again, little Fort George. These forts were held by about 1,800 British, mostly American colonists, with 123 guns of all kinds.

While it was still dark Montcalm gave out his orders. At the first streak of dawn the Indians and Canadians were in position to protect the engineers and working parties. Only one accident marred the success of the opening day. One of the French engineers was returning to camp through the woods at dusk, when an Indian, mistaking him for an enemy, shot him dead. It is said that this Indian felt so sorry for what he had done that he vowed to avenge the engineer's loss on the British, and did not stop scalp-hunting during the rest of the war; but went on until he had lifted as many as thirty scalps from the hated British heads. In the meantime, other engineers had traced out the road from the bay to the battery. Led by their officers the French regulars set to work with such goodwill that the road was ready next day for the siege train of twenty-two cannon, now landed in the nick of time.

Every part of the siege was made to fit in perfectly with every other part. While the guns were being landed, the British, who had only just taken alarm, sent round two armed vessels to stop this work. But Montcalm had placed a battery all ready to beat off an attack, and the landing went on like clockwork. The next day, again, the soldiers were as busy as bees round the doomed British forts. Canadians and Indians filled the woods. Canadians and French hauled the cannon up to the battery commanding Fort Ontario, but left them hidden nearby till after dark. The engineers made the first parallel. French troops raised the battery; and at daylight the next morning it was ready. Fort Ontario kept up an active fire, at a distance of only a musket shot, two hundred yards; but the French fire was so furious that the British guns were silenced the same afternoon.

Colonel Mercer, the British commander, called in the garrison, who abandoned Fort Ontario and crossed the river after spiking the guns. Without a moment's delay Montcalm seized the fort and kept his working parties hauling guns all night long. In the morning Fort Oswego on the other side of the river was commanded by a heavier battery than the one that had taken Fort Ontario the day before. More than this, the Canadians and Indians had crossed the river and had cut off the little Fort George, half a mile beyond. There was a stiff fight for it, but Mercer's men were driven off into the other fort with considerable loss.

Montcalm's new battery beside the river was on higher ground than Fort Oswego, which was only five hundred yards away. At six o'clock it opened fire and ploughed up the whole area of the fort with terrible effect. Hardly a spot was left which the French shells did not search out. The British reply, fired uphill, soon began to falter. The French fire was redoubled. Colonel Mercer was killed by a cannon

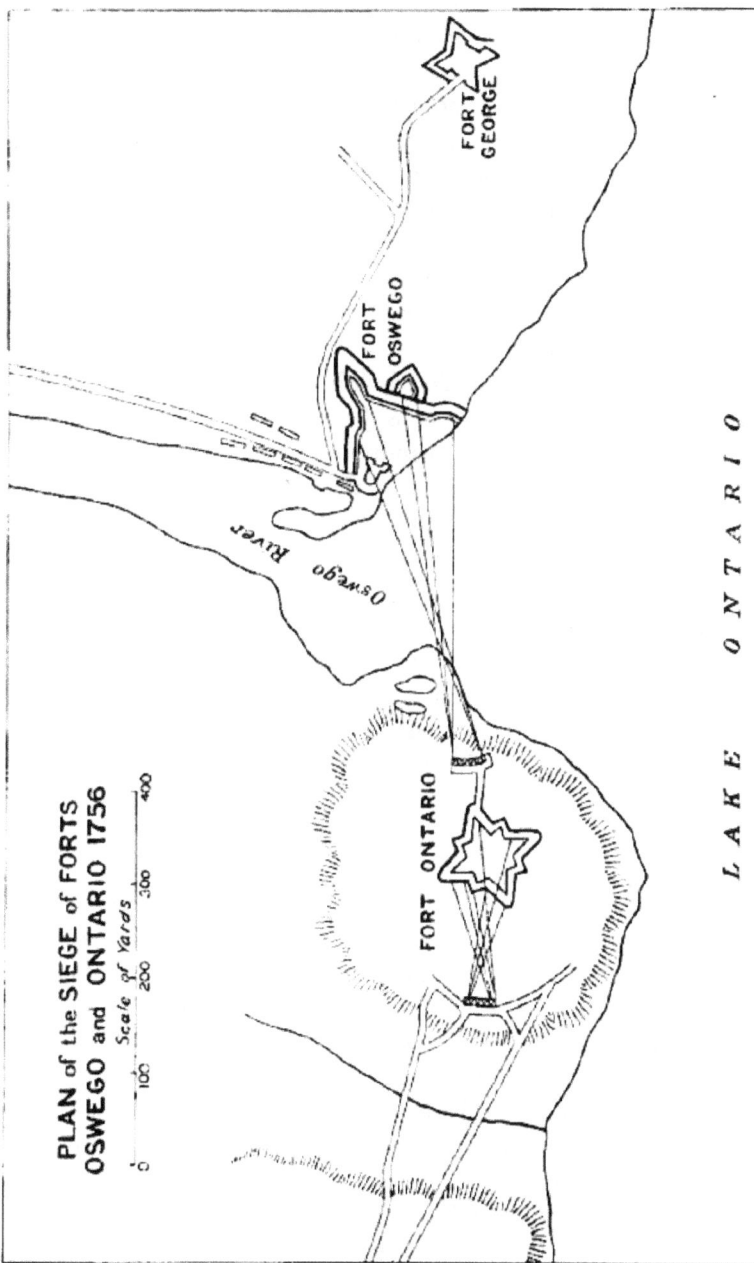

PLAN of the SIEGE of FORTS OSWEGO and ONTARIO 1756

Scale of Yards
0   100   200   300   400

FORT GEORGE

FORT OSWEGO

Oswego River

FORT ONTARIO

LAKE ONTARIO

ball, and this, of course, weakened the British defence, The second-in-command kept up the unequal fight for another couple of hours. Then, finding that he could not induce his men to face the murderous fire any longer, and seeing his fort cut off by land and water, he ran up the white flag.

Montcalm gave him an hour to surrender both fort and garrison. Again there was no time to lose, and again Montcalm lost none. That morning a letter found on a British messenger showed that Colonel Webb, with 2,000 men, was somewhere up the river Oswego waiting for news. So, while Montcalm was attacking the fort with his batteries, he was also preparing his army to attack Webb. He did not intend to wait; but to march out and meet the new enemy, so as not to be caught between two fires.

At eleven the fort surrendered with 1,600 prisoners, 123 cannon, powder, shot, stores and provisions of all kinds; 5 armed ships and 200 boats. There was also a large quantity of wine and rum, which Montcalm at once spilt into the lake, lest the Indians should get hold of it and in their drunken frenzy begin a massacre. As it was, they were anything but pleased to find that he was conducting the war on European principles, and that he would not let them scalp the sick and wounded British. Some of them sneaked in and, in the first confusion, took a few scalps. But Montcalm was among them at once and stopped them short. He had been warned not to offend them; and so he promised them rich presents if they would behave properly. In his dispatch to the minister of War he said: 'I am afraid my promises will cost ten thousand *francs*; but the keeping of them will attach the Indians more to our side. In any case, there is nothing I would not have done to prevent any breach of faith with the enemy.'

In a single week every part of all three forts was levelled with the ground. This delighted the Indians more than anything else, for they rightly feared that any British advance in this direction would be sure to end in their being driven out of their own country. By August 21, ten days from the time the first shot was fired, Montcalm was leading his victorious army back to Montreal.

The news spread like wildfire. No such sudden, complete, and surprising victory had ever before been won in the West. The name and fame of Montcalm ran along the war-paths of the endless forest and passed from mouth to mouth over ten thousand leagues of inland waters. In one short summer the magic of that single word, Montcalm, became as great in America as it had been for centuries in France. The whole face of the war was changed. At the beginning of the year the British had thought of nothing but attack. Then, when Montcalm had shown them so bold a front at Ticonderoga, they had paused to make sure. Now, after Oswego, they thought of nothing but defence.

People could hardly believe that one and the same man had in July checked the threatened British invasion at Lake Champlain and in August had taken the stronghold of British power on Lake Ontario. Every step of the way had to be covered by force of the men's own legs and arms, marching, paddling, hauling, carrying. In short, Montcalm had moved a whole army, siege train and all, as fast through the wilderness without horses as another army would have been moved over good roads in Europe with them. The wonder grew when the numbers became known. With 3,000 men and 22 guns Montcalm had taken three forts with a garrison of 1,800 men and 123 guns; and had done this in face of five armed British vessels against his own two, and in spite of the fact that 2,000 more British soldiers were close behind him in the forest.

Canada burst into great rejoicings. All the churches sang *Te Deum*. The five captured flags were carried in triumph through Montreal, Three Rivers, and Quebec. In France the news was received with great jubilation, and many of Montcalm's officers gained promotion. In the midst of all this glory Montcalm was busy looking after the health and comfort of his men, seeing that the Canadians were sent home as soon as possible to gather in their harvest, and engaging the Indians to join him for a still greater war next year. Nor did he forget anyone who had done him faithful service. He asked, as a special favour, that an old sergeant, Marcel, who had come out as his orderly and clerk, should be made a captain. Marcel had thus good reason never to forget Montcalm. It was his hand that wrote the last letter which Montcalm ever dictated and signed, the one to the British commander after the battle of the Plains, the one which admitted the ultimate failure of all Montcalm's heroic work.

Another man whom Montcalm specially praised was Bougainville, his *aide-de-camp*, of whom we shall hear again very often. Bougainville, though still under thirty, was already a well-known man of science who had been made a Fellow of the Royal Society of London. 'You could hardly believe how full of resource he is,' wrote the admiring Montcalm, who then added modestly:

As the account of this expedition may be printed I have asked him to correct it carefully, because he writes much better than I do.

Only one thing spoiled the triumph; and that was the jealousy of Vaudreuil, who tried to claim all the credit of making the plan for himself and the credit of carrying it out for the Canadians. Certainly he had been saying for some time before Montcalm arrived that Oswego ought to be taken. Everybody on both sides knew perfectly well, however, that Oswego was the gateway of the West; so Vaudreuil was not a bit wiser than many others. In a way he did make the plan. But Montcalm was the one who really worked it out. Vaudreuil pressed the button that launched the ship. It was Montcalm who took her into action and brought her out victorious.

Montcalm's crew worked well together. But this did not suit Vaudreuil at all. He wrote both to the Minister of War and to the minister of Marine in France, praising the Canadians and Indians and making as little as possible of the work of the French.

The French regulars showed their wonted zeal; but the enemy did not give them a chance to do much work.

Our troops, the Canadians and Indians, fought with courage. They have all done very well.

True enough. But, all the same, the regulars were, from first to last, the backbone of the defence of Canada.

The measures I took made our victory certain. If I had been less firm, Oswego would still have been in the hands of the British. I cannot sufficiently congratulate myself on the zeal which my brother (an officer in the Canadian service) and the Canadians and Indians showed. Without them my orders would have been given in vain.

And so on, and so on.

Montcalm saw the real strength and weakness of the Canadians and wrote his own opinion to the Minister of War.

Our French regulars did all I required with splendid zeal. . . . I made good use of the militia, but not at the works exposed to the enemy's fire. These militiamen have no discipline. In six months I could make grenadiers of them. But at present I would not rely on them, nor believe what they say about themselves; for they think themselves quite the finest fellows in the world.

The governor is a native of Canada, was married here, and is surrounded by his relatives on all sides.

The fact is that the war was no longer an affair of little raids, first on one side and then on the other, but was becoming, more and more, a war on a great scale, with long campaigns, larger numbers of men, trains of artillery, fortifications, and all the other things that require well-drilled troops who have thoroughly learned the soldier's duty, and are ready to do it at any time and in any place. War is like everything else in the world. The men whose regular business it is will wage it better than the men who only do it as an odd job. Of course, if the best men are chosen for the militia, and the worst are turned into regulars, the militia may beat the regulars, even on equal terms. If, too, regulars are set down in a strange country, quite unlike the one in which they have been trained to fight, naturally they will begin by making a good many mistakes. But, for all-round work, the same men, as regulars, are worth much more than twice what they are worth as militia, everywhere and always.

CHAPTER 4

Fort William Henry 1757

In January Montcalm paid a visit to Quebec, and there began to see how Bigot and his fellow-vampires were sucking away the life-blood of Canada.

> The *intendant* lives in grandeur, and has given two splendid balls, where I have seen over eighty very charming and well-dressed ladies. I think Quebec is a town of very good style, and I do not believe we have a dozen cities in France that could rank before it as a social centre.

This was well enough; though not when armies were only half-fed. But here is the real crime:

> The *intendant's* strong taste for gambling, and the governor's weakness in letting him have his own way, are causing a great deal of play for very high stakes. Many officers will repent it soon and bitterly.

Montcalm was placed in a most awkward position. He wished to stop the ruinous gambling. But he was under Vaudreuil, had no power over the *intendant*, and, as he said himself, 'felt obliged not to oppose either of them in public, because they were invested with the king's authority.'

Vaudreuil nearly did Canada a very good turn this winter, by falling ill on his way to Montreal. But, luckily for the British and unluckily for the French, he recovered. On February 14 he began hatching more mischief. The British, having been stopped in the West at Oswego, were certain to try another advance, in greater force, by the centre, up Lake Champlain. The French, with fewer men and very much less provisions and stores of all kinds, could hope to win only by giving the British another sudden, smashing blow and then keeping them in check for the rest of the summer. The whole strength of Canada was needed to give this blow, and every pound of food was precious. Vaudreuil, however, was planning to take separate action on his own account. He organized a raid under his brother, Rigaud, without telling Montcalm a word about it till the whole plan was made, even though the raid required the use of some of the French regulars, who were, in an especial degree, under Montcalm's command. Montcalm told Vaudreuil that it was a pity not to keep their whole strength for one decisive dash, and that, if this raid was to take place at all, Levis or some other regular French officer high in rank should be in command.

Vaudreuil, however, adhered to his own plan. This time there was to be no question of credit for anyone but Canadians, Indians, Vaudreuil himself, and his brother. As for making sure of victory by taking, as Montcalm advised, a really strong force: well, Vaudreuil would trust to luck, hit or miss, as he always had trusted before. And a strange stroke of luck very nearly did serve his unworthy turn. For, on March 17, when the 1,600 raiders were drawing quite close to Fort William Henry, most of the little British garrison of 400 men were drinking so much New England rum in honour of St Patrick's Day that their muskets would have hurt friends more than foes if an attack had been made that night. Next evening the French crept up, hoping to surprise the place. But the sentries were once more alert. Through the silence they heard a tapping noise on the lake, which turned out to be made by a Canadian who was trying the strength of the ice with the back of his axe to see if it would bear. This led to a brisk defence. When the French advanced over the ice the British gunners sent such a hail of grape-shot crashing along this precarious foothold that the enemy were glad to scamper off as hard as their legs would take them.

The French did not abandon their attempt, however, and two days later Vaudreuil's brother arrayed his 1,600 men against the fort and summoned it to surrender. As he had no guns the garrison would not listen to him. Rigaud then proceeded to burn what he could outside the fort. He certainly made a splendid bonfire; the wild, red flames leaped into the sky from the open, snow-white clearings beside the fort, with the long, white reaches of Lake George in front and the dark, densely wooded hills all round. A great deal was burnt: four small ships, 350 boats, a sawmill, sheds, magazines, immense piles of firewood, and a large supply of provisions. But the British could afford this loss much better than the French could afford the cost of the raid. And the cost, of course, was five times as great as it ought to have been. Bigot's gang took care of that.

Then the raiders, unable to take the fort, set out for home on snow-shoes. There had been a very heavy snowstorm before they started, and the spring sun was now shining full on the glaring white snow. Many of them, even among the Canadians and Indians, were struck snowblind so badly that they had to be led by the hand—no easy thing on snow-shoes. At the end of March they were safely back in Montreal, where Vaudreuil and his brother went strutting about like a pair of turkey-cocks.

Montcalm's first Canadian winter wore away. Vaudreuil and Bigot still kept up an outward politeness in all their relations with him. But they were beginning to fear that he was far too wise and honest for them. He was, however, under Vaudreuil's foolish orders and he had no power to check Bigot's knaveries. Much against his will he was already getting into debt, and was thus rendered even more helpless. Vaudreuil, as governor, had plenty of money. Bigot stole as much as he wished. But Montcalm was not well paid. Yet, as the commander-in-chief, he had to be asking people to dinners and receptions almost every day, while becoming less and less able to meet the expense. The Bigot gang made provisions so scarce and so dear that only the thieves themselves could pay for them. Well might the sorely tried general write home: 'What a country, where knaves grow rich and honest men are ruined!'

In June there was such a sight in Montreal as Canada had never seen before, and never saw again. During the autumn, the winter, and the spring, messengers had been going along every warpath and waterway, east and west for thousands of miles, to summon the tribes to meet Onontio; as they called the French governor, at Montreal. The ice had hardly gone in April when the first of the braves began to arrive in flotillas of bark canoes. The surrender of Washington at Fort Necessity and the capture and rebuilding of Fort Duquesne in 1754, the bloody defeat of Braddock in 1755, and Montcalm's sudden, smashing blow against Oswego in 1756, all had led the western Indians to think that the French were everything and the British nothing.

In Canada itself the Indians were equally sure that the French were going to be the victors there; while in the east, in far Acadia, the Abnakis were as bitter as the Acadians themselves against the British. So now, whether eager for more victories or thirsting for revenge, the warriors came to Montreal from far and near.

Fifty-one of the tribes were ready for the warpath. Their chiefs had sat in grave debate round the council fires. Their medicine men had made charms in secret *wigwams* and seen visions of countless British scalps and piles of British booty. Accordingly, when the braves of these fifty-one tribes met at Montreal, there was war in every heart among them. No town in the world had ever shown more startling contrasts in its streets. Here, side by side, were outward signs of the highest civilization and of the lowest barbarism. Here were the most refined of ladies, dressed in the latest Paris fashions, mincing about in silks and satins and high-heeled, golden-buckled shoes. Here were the most courtly gentlemen of Europe, in the same embroidered and beruffled uniforms that they would have worn before the king of France. Yet in and out of this gay throng of polite society went hundreds of copper-coloured braves; some of them more than half-naked; most of them ready, after a victory, to be cannibals who revelled in stews of white man's flesh; all of them decked in waving plumes, all of them grotesquely painted, like demons in a nightmare, and all of them armed to the teeth.

Much to Vaudreuil's disgust the man whom the Indians wished most to see was not himself, the 'Great Onontio,' much less Bigot, prince of thieves, but the warrior chief, Montcalm. They had the good sense to prefer the lion to the owl or the fox. Three hundred of the wildest Ottawas came striding in one day, each man a model of agility and strength, a living bronze, a sculptor's dream, the whole making a picture for the brush of the greatest painter. 'We want to see the chief who tramples the British to death and sweeps their forts off the face of the earth.' Montcalm, though every inch a soldier, was rather short than tall; and at first the Ottawa chief looked surprised. 'We thought your head would be lost in the clouds,' he said. But then, as he caught Montcalm's piercing glance, he added: 'Yet when we look into your eyes, we see the height of the pine and the wings of the eagle.'

Meanwhile, prisoners, scouts, and spies had been coming in; so too had confidential dispatches from France confirming the rumours that the greater part of the British army was to attack Louisbourg, and that the French were well able to defend it. With the British concentrating their strength on Louisbourg a chance offered for another Oswego-like blow against the British forts at the southern end of Lake George if it could be made by July. But Vaudreuil's raid in March, and Bigot's bill for it, had eaten up so much of the supplies and money, that nothing like a large force could be made ready to strike before August; and the month's delay might give the militia of the British colonies, slow as they were, time to be brought up to the help of the forts.

Montcalm was now eager to strike the blow. Once clear of Montreal and its gang of parasites, he soon had his motley army in hand, in spite of all kinds of difficulties. In May Bourlamaque had begun rebuilding Ticonderoga. In July Lake Champlain began to swarm with boats, canoes, and sailing vessels, all moving south towards the doomed fort on Lake George. Montcalm's whole force numbered 8,000. Of these 3,000 were regulars, 3,000 were militia, and 2,000 were Indians from the fifty-one different tribes, very few of whom knew anything of war, except war as it was carried on by savages. By the end of the month these 8,000 men were camped along the four miles of valley between Lakes Champlain and George. Meanwhile the British were at the other end of Lake George, little more than thirty miles away. Their first post was Fort William Henry, where they had 2,200 men under Colonel Monro. Fourteen miles inland beyond that was Fort Edward, where Webb commanded 3,600 men.

There were 900 more British troops still farther on, but well within call, and it was known that a large force of militia were being assembled somewhere near Albany. Thus Montcalm knew that the British already had nearly as many men as his own regulars and militia put together, and that further levies of militia might come on at any time and in any numbers. He therefore had to strike as hard and fast as he could, and then retire on Ticonderoga. He knew the Indians would go home at once after the fight and also that he must send the Canadians home in August to save their harvest. Then he would be left with only 3,000 regulars, who could not be fed for the rest of the summer so far from headquarters. With this 3,000 he could not advance, in any case, because of lack of food and because of the presence of Webb's 4,500, increased by an unknown number of American militia.

The first skirmish on Lake George was fought while the main bodies of both armies were still at opposite ends. A party of 400 Indians and 50 Canadians were paddling south when they saw advancing on the lake a number of British boats with 300 men, mostly raw militia from New Jersey. The Indians went ashore and hid. The doomed militiamen rowed on in careless, straggling disorder. Suddenly, as they passed a wooded point, the calm air was rent with blood-curdling war-whoops, and the lake seemed alive with red-skinned fiends, who paddled in among the British boats in one bewildering moment. The militiamen were seized with a panic and tried to escape. But they could not get away from the finest paddlers in the world, who cut them off, upset their boats, tomahawked some, and speared a good many others like fish in the water. Only two boats, out of twenty-three, escaped to tell the tale. That night the forest resounded with savage yells of triumph as the prisoners, out of reach of all help from either army, were killed and scalped to the last man.

On August 1 Montcalm advanced by land and water. He sent Levis by land with 3,000 men to cut Fort William Henry off from Fort Edward, while he went himself, with the rest of his army, by water in boats and canoes. The next day they met at a little bay quite close to the fort. On the 3rd the final advance was made. The French canoes formed lines stretching right across the lake. While the artillery was being landed in a cove out of reach of the guns of the fort Levis was having a lively skirmish with the British, who were trying to drive in their cattle and save their tents. About 500 of them held the fort, and 1,700 were in the entrenched camp some way beyond.

Montcalm sent in a summons to surrender. But old Colonel Monro replied that he was ready to fight. On the 4th and 5th the French batteries rose as if by magic. But the Indians, not used to the delay and the careful preparation which a siege involves, soon grew angry and impatient, and swarmed all over the French lines, asking why they were ordered here and there and treated like slaves, why their advice had not been sought, and why the big guns were not being fired. Montcalm had been counselled to humour them as much as possible and on no account whatever to offend them. Their help was needed, and the British were quite ready to win them over to their own side if possible.

Accordingly, on the afternoon of the 5th, Montcalm held a grand 'pow-wow' with the savages. He told them that the French had to be slow at first, but that the very next day the big guns would begin to fire, and that they would all be in the fight together. The fort was timbered and made a good target. The Indians greeted the first roar of the siege guns with yells of delight; and when they saw shells bursting and scattering earth and timbers in all directions they shrieked and whooped so loudly that their savage voices woke almost as many wild echoes along those beautiful shores as the thunder of the guns themselves.

Presently a man came in to the French camp with a letter addressed to Monro, which the Indians had found concealed in a hollow

SIEGE OF
FORT WILLIAM HENRY
1757

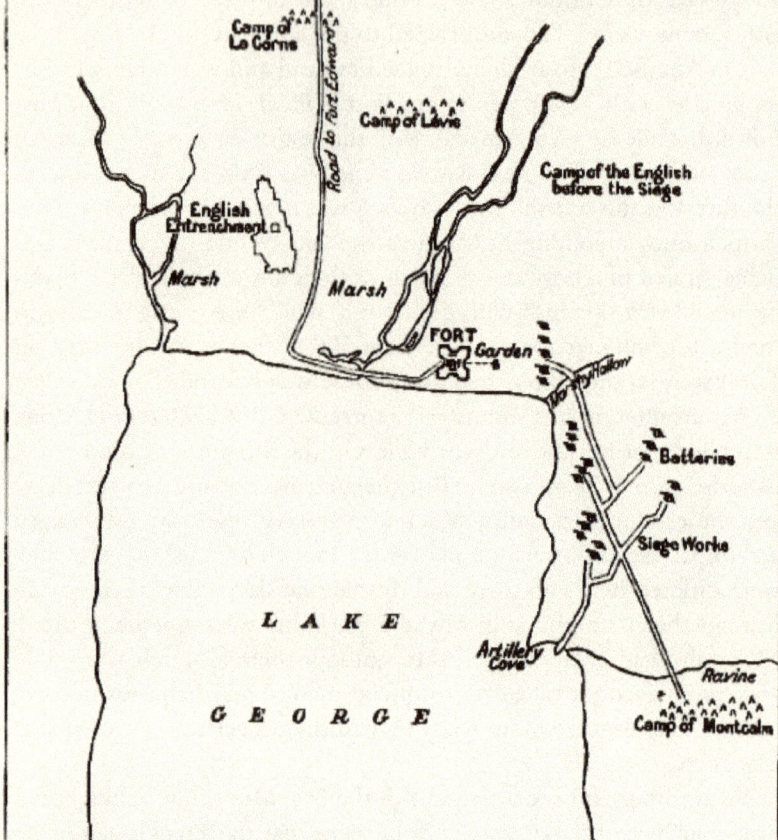

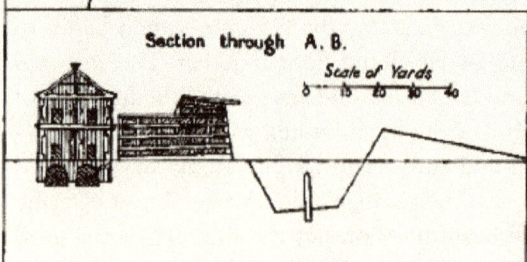

Camp of
Le Corns

Road to Fort Edward

Camp of Lévis

Camp of the English
before the Siege

English
Entrenchment

Marsh

Marsh

FORT

Garden

Woody Hollow

Batteries

Siege Works

Artillery
Cove

L A K E

G E O R G E

Ravine

Camp of Montcalm

Section through A. B.

Scale of Yards

0   15   20   30   40

bullet on a British messenger whom they had killed. This letter was from Monro's superior officer, General Webb, fourteen miles distant at Fort Edward. He advised Monro to make the best terms possible with Montcalm, as he did not feel strong enough to relieve Fort William Henry. Montcalm stopped his batteries and sent the letter in to Monro by Bougainville, with his compliments. But Monro, while thanking him for his courtesy, still said he should hold out to the last.

Montcalm now decided to bring matters to a head at once. As yet his batteries were too far off to be effective, and between them and the fort lay first a marsh and then a little hill. By sheer hard work the French made a road for their cannon across the marsh; and Monro saw, to his horror, that Montcalm's new batteries were rising, in spite of the British fire, right opposite the fort, on top of the little hill, and only two hundred and fifty yards away.

Monro knew he was lost. Smallpox was raging in the fort. Webb would not move. Montcalm was able to knock the whole place to pieces and destroy the garrison. On the 9th the white flag went up. Montcalm granted the honours of war. The British were to march off the next morning to Fort Edward, carrying their arms, and under escort of a body of French regulars. Every precaution was taken to keep the Indians from committing any outrage. Montcalm assembled them, told them the terms, and persuaded them to promise obedience. He took care to keep all strong drink out of their way, and asked Monro to destroy all the liquor in the British fort and camp.

In spite of these precautions a dire tragedy followed. While the garrison were marching out of the fort towards their own camp, some Indians climbed in without being seen and began to scalp the sick and wounded who were left behind in charge of the French. The French guard, hearing cries, rushed in and stopped the savages by force. The British were partly to blame for this first outrage: they had not poured out the rum, and the Indians had stolen enough to make them drunk. Montcalm came down himself, at the first alarm, and did his utmost. He seized and destroyed all the liquor; and he arranged with two chiefs from each tribe to be ready to start in the morning with the armed British and their armed escort. He went back to his tent only at nine o'clock, when everything was quiet.

Much worse things happened the next morning. The British, who had some women and children with them, and who still kept a good deal of rum in their canteens, began to stir much earlier than had been arranged. The French escort had not arrived when the British column began to straggle out on the road to Fort Edward. When the march began the scattered column was two or three times as long as it ought to have been. Meanwhile a savage enemy was on the alert. Before daylight the Abnakis of Acadia, who hated the British most of all, had slunk off unseen to prepare an ambush for the first stragglers they could find. Other Indians, who had appeared later, had begged for rum from the British, who had given it in the hope that, in this way, they might be got rid of. Suddenly, a war-whoop was raised, a wild rush on the British followed, and a savage massacre began. The British column, long and straggling already, broke up, and the French escort could defend only those who kept together.

At the first news Montcalm ordered out another guard, and himself rushed with all his staff officers to the scene of outrage. They ran every risk to save their prisoners from massacre. Several French officers and soldiers were wounded by the savages, and all did their best. The Canadians, on the other hand, more hardened to Indian ways, simply looked on at the wild scene. Most of the British were rescued and were taken safely to Fort Edward. The French fired cannon from Fort William Henry to guide fugitives back. Those not massacred at once, but made prisoners by the Indians in the woods, were in nearly all cases ransomed by Vaudreuil, who afterwards sent them to Halifax in a French ship.

Such was the 'massacre of Fort William Henry,' about which people took opposite views at the time, as they do still. It is quite clear that, in the first instance, Montcalm did almost everything that any man in his place could possibly do to protect his captives from the Indians. It is also clear that he did everything possible during and after the massacre, even to risking his life and the lives of his officers and men. He might, indeed, have turned out all his French regulars to guard the captive column from the first. But there were only 2,500 of these regulars, not many more than the British, who were armed, who ought to have poured out every drop of rum the night before, and who ought to have started only at the proper time and in proper order. There were faults on both sides, as there usually are. But, except for not having the whole of his regulars ready at the spot, which did not seem necessary the night before, Montcalm stands quite clear of all blame as a general. His efforts to stop the bloody work—and they were successful efforts involving danger to himself—clear him of all blame as a man.

The number of persons massacred has been given by some few

British and American writers as amounting to 1,500. Most people know now that this is nonsense. All but about a hundred of the losses on the British side are accounted for otherwise, under the heading of those who were either killed in battle, or died of sickness, or were given up at Fort Edward, or were sent back by way of Halifax. It is simply impossible that more than a hundred were massacred.

Still, a massacre is a massacre; all sorts of evil are sure to come of it; and this one was no exception to the rule. It blackened unjustly the good name of Montcalm. It led to an intensely bitter hate of the British against the Canadians, many of whom were given no quarter afterwards. It caused the British to break the terms of surrender, which required the prisoners not to fight again for the next eighteen months. Most of all, the massacre hurt the Indians, guilty and innocent alike. Many of them took scalps from men who had smallpox; and so they carried this dread disease throughout the wilderness, where it killed fifty times as many of their own people as they had killed on the British side.

The massacre at Fort William Henry raises the whole vexed question of the rights of the savages and of their means of defence. The Indians naturally wished to live in their own country in their own way—as other people do. They did not like the whites to push them aside—who does like being pushed aside? But, if they had to choose between different nations of whites, they naturally chose the ones who changed their country the least. Now, the British colonists were aggressive and numerous; and they were always taking more and more land from the Indians, in one way or another. The French, on the other hand, were few, they wanted less of the land, for they were more inclined to trade than to farm, and in general they managed to get on with the Indians better.

Therefore most of the Indians took sides with the French; and therefore most of the scalps lifted were British scalps. The question of the barbarity of Indian warfare remains. The Indians were in fact living the same sort of barbarous life that the ancestors of the French and British had lived two or three thousand years earlier. So the Indians did, of course, just what the French and the British would have done at a corresponding age. Peoples take centuries to grow into civilized nations; and it is absurd to expect savages to change more in a hundred years than Europeans changed in a thousand.

We need hardly inquire which side was the more right and which the more wrong in respect to these barbarities. The fact is, there were plenty of rights and wrongs all round. Each side excused itself and accused the other. The pot has always called the kettle black. Both the French and the British made use of Indians when the savages themselves would gladly have remained neutral. In contrast with the colonial levies the French and British regulars, trained in European discipline, were less inclined to 'act the Indian'; but both did so on occasion. The French regulars did a little scalping on their own account now and then; the Canadian regulars did more than a little; while the Canadian militiamen, roughened by their many raids, did a great deal.

The first thing Wolfe's regulars did at Louisbourg was to scalp an Indian chief. The American rangers were scalpers when their blood was up and when nobody stopped them. They scalped under Wolfe at Quebec. They scalped whites as well as Indians at Baie St Paul, at St Joachim, and elsewhere. Even Washington was a party to such practices. When sending in a batch of Indian scalps for the usual reward offered by Governor Dinwiddie of Virginia he asked that an extra one might be paid for at the usual rate, 'although it is not an Indian's.' It is thus clear that the barbarities were in effect a normal feature of warfare in the wilderness.

A week after its surrender Fort William Henry had been wiped off the face of the earth, as Oswego had been the year before, and Montcalm's army had set out homeward bound. But he was sick at heart. Vaudreuil had been behaving worse than ever. He had written and ordered Montcalm to push on and take Fort Edward at once. Yet, as we have seen, the Indians had melted away, the Canadians had gone home for the harvest, only 3,000 regulars were left, and these could not be kept a month longer in the field for lack of food. In spite of this, Vaudreuil thought Montcalm ought to advance into British territory, besiege a larger army than his own, and beat it in spite of all the British militia that were coming to its aid.

Even before leaving for the front Montcalm had written to France asking to be recalled from Canada. In this letter to the minister of Marine he spoke very freely. He pointed out that if Vaudreuil had died in the winter the new governor would have been Rigaud, Vaudreuil's brother. What this would have meant everyone knew only too well; for Rigaud was a still bigger fool than Vaudreuil himself. Montcalm gave the Canadians their due. 'What a people, when called upon! They have talent and courage enough, but nobody has called these qualities forth.' In fact, the wretched Canadian was bullied and also flattered by

Vaudreuil, robbed by Bigot, bothered on his farm by all kinds of foolish regulations, and then expected to be a model subject and soldier. How could he be considered a soldier when he had never been anything but a mere raider, not properly trained, not properly armed, not properly fed, and not paid at all?

While Montcalm was writing the truth Vaudreuil was writing lie after lie about Montcalm, in order to do him all the harm he could. Busy tell-tales repeated and twisted every impatient word Montcalm spoke, and altogether Canada was at sixes and sevens. Vaudreuil, sitting comfortably at his desk and eating three good meals a day, had written to Montcalm saying that there would be no trouble about provisions if Fort Edward was attacked. Yet, at this very time, he had given orders that, because of scarcity, the Canadians at home should not have more than a quarter of a pound of bread a day. Canada was drawing very near a famine, though its soil could grow some of the finest crops in the world. But what can any country do under knaves and fools, especially when it is gagged as well as robbed? Montcalm's complaints did not always reach the minister of Marine, who was the special person in France to look after Canada; for the minister's own right-hand man was one of the Bigot gang and knew how to steal a letter as well as a shipload of stores.

To outward view, and especially in the eyes of the British Americans, 1757 was a year of nothing but triumph for the French in America. They had made Louisbourg safer than ever; the British fleet and army had not even dared to attack it. French power had never been so widespread. The *fleurs-de-lis* floated over the whole of the valleys of the St Lawrence, Ohio, and Mississippi, as well as over the Great Lakes, where these three valleys meet. But this great show of strength depended on the army of Montcalm—that motley host behind whose dauntless front everything was hollow and rotten to the last degree. The time was soon to come when even the bravest of armies could no longer stand against lions in front and jackals behind.

CHAPTER 5

Ticonderoga 1758

Montcalm's second winter in Canada was worse than his first. Vaudreuil, Bigot, and all the men in the upper circles of what would nowadays be the business, the political, and the official world, lived on the fat of the land; but the rest only on what fragments were left. In our meaning of the word 'business' there was in reality no business at all. There were then no real merchants in Canada, no real tradesmen, no bankers, no shippers, no honest men of affairs at all. Everything was done by or under the government, and the government was controlled by or under the Bigot gang. This gang stole a great deal of what was found in Canada, and most of what came out from France as well. In consequence, supplies became scarcer and scarcer and dearer and dearer; and the worst of it was that the gang wished things to be scarce and dear, so that more stores and money might be sent out from France and stolen on arrival. For France, in spite of all her faults in governing, helped Canada, and helped her generously.

It seems too terrible for belief, but it is true that the parasites in Canada did their best on this account to keep the people half starved. Montcalm saw through the scheme, but complaint was almost useless, for many of his letters were stopped before they reached the head men in France. To cap all, the wretched army was no longer paid in gold, which always has its own fixed value, but in paper bills which had no real money to back them, as banknotes have today. The result was that this money was accepted at much less than its face value, and that every officer who had to support himself, as he must when not campaigning, fell into debt, Montcalm, of course, more than the others. 'What a country,' to repeat his words, 'where knaves grow rich and honest men are ruined!'

As the winter wore away food grew scarcer—except for those who belonged to the gang. Soldiers were allowed about a pound of meat a day. This would have been luxury if the meat had been good, and if they had had anything else to eat with it. But a pound of bad beef, or of scraggy horse-flesh, or sometimes even of flabby salt cod-fish, with a quarter of a pound of bread, and nothing else but a little Indian corn, is not a good ration for an army. The Canadians were worse off still. In the spring the bread ration was halved again, and became only a couple of ounces. Two thousand Acadians had escaped from the British efforts to deport them, and had reached the St Lawrence region. Their needs increased the misery, for they could not yet grow as much as they ate, even if they had had a fair chance.

At last the poor, patient, down-trodden Canadians began to grumble. One day a crowd of angry women threw their horse-flesh at Vaudreuil's door. Another day even the grenadiers refused to eat their rations. Then Montcalm's second-in-command, Levis, who ate horse-flesh himself, for the sake of example, told them that Canada was now like a besieged fortress and that the garrison would have to put up with hardships. At once the pride of the soldier came out. Next day they brought him some roast horse, better cooked and served than his own. He gave each grenadier a gold coin to drink the king's health; and the trouble ended.

The Canadians and Indians made two successful raids. One was against a place near Schenectady, where they destroyed many stores and provisions. The other ended in a fight with the British guerilla leader Rogers and his rangers, who were badly cut up near Ticonderoga. The Canadians were at their best in making raids. Yet now raids hardly counted any longer, for the war had outgrown them. Larger and larger armies were taking the field, and these armies had artillery, engineers, and transport on a greater scale. The mere raider, or odd-job soldier, though always good in his own place and in his own kind of country, was becoming less and less important compared with the regular. The larger an army the more the difference of value widens between regulars and militia. In great wars men must be trained to act together at any time, in any place, and in any numbers; and this is only possible with those all-the-year-round soldiers who are either regulars already or who, though militia to start with, become by practice the same as regulars.

When Montcalm looked forward to the campaign of 1758, he saw in what a desperate plight he was. The wild, unstable Indians were the weakest element. Gladly would he have done without them altogether. But some were always needed as scouts and guides; and, in any case, it was a good thing to employ them so as to keep them from joining the enemy. The trouble was that they were already beginning to fail him. Some of the ships with goods for the Indians were captured by the British fleet. Those that arrived were in as real a sense captured, for they were stolen by the Bigot gang, and did not fulfil the purpose of holding the Indian allies. 'If,' said Montcalm, in one of his despairing letters to the minister, 'if all the presents that the king sends out to the Indians were really given to them, we should have every tribe in America on our own side.'

The Canadians were robbed even more; and they and the Canadian regulars were set against Montcalm and the French by every lie that Vaudreuil could speak in Canada or write to France. The wonder is, not that the French Canadians of those dreadful days did badly now and then, but that they did so well on the whole; that they were so brave, so loyal, so patient, so hopeful, so true to many of the best traditions of their race. One other feature of their system must be noted—the influence of their priests. Protestants would think them too much under the thumb of the priests. But, however this may have been, it can be said with truth that the church and the native soldiers, with all their faults, were the glory of Canada, while the government was nothing but its shame. The priests stood by their people like men, suffered hardship with them, and helped them to face every trial of fortune against false friends and open foes alike.

The mainstay of the defence of Canada was, however, the disciplined strength of the French regulars. There were eight battalions, belonging to seven regiments whose names deserve to be held in honour wherever the fight for Canada is known: La Reine, Guienne, Bearn, Languedoc, La Sarre, Royal Roussillon, and Berry. Each battalion had about 500 fighting men, making about 4,000 in all. About 2,000 more men were sent out to Quebec to fill up gaps at different times; so that, one way and another, at least 6,000 French soldiers reached Canada between 1755 and 1759. Yet, when Levis laid down the arms of France in Canada for ever in 1760, only 2,000 of all these remained. About 1,000 had been taken prisoner on sea or land. A few had deserted. But almost 3,000 had been lost by sickness or in battle. How many armies have a record of sacrifices greater than these, and against foes behind as well as in front?

From the very first these gallant men showed their mettle. They were not forced to go to Canada. They went willingly. When the first

LÉVIS

four battalions went, the general who had to arrange their departure was afraid he might have trouble in filling the gaps by getting men to volunteer from the other battalions of the same regiments. But no. He could have filled every gap ten times over. It was the same with the officers. Everyone was eager to fight for the honour of France in Canada. One officer actually offered his whole fortune to another, in hopes of getting this other's place for service in Canada. But in vain. France had parasites at court, plenty of them. But the French troops who went out were patriots almost to a man. The only exception was in the case we have noticed before, when 400 riff-raff were sent out to take the places of the 400 good men whom Boscawen had captured in the Gulf during the summer of 1755.

The year 1758 saw the tide turn against France. Pitt was now at the head of the war in Britain; throughout the British Empire the patriots had gained the upper hand over the parasites. Canada could no longer attack; indeed, she was hard pressed for defence. Pitt's plan was to send one army against the west, a fleet and an army against the east at Louisbourg, and a third army straight at the centre, along the line of Lake Champlain. This third, or central, army was the one which Montcalm had to meet. It was the largest yet seen in the New World. There were 6,000 British regulars and 9,000 American militia, with plenty of guns and all the other arms and stores required. Its general, Abercromby, was its chief weakness. He was a muddle-headed man, whom Pitt had not yet been able to replace by a better. But Lord Howe, whom Wolfe and Pitt both thought 'a perfect model of military virtue,' was second-in-command and the real head. He was young, as full of calm wisdom as of fiery courage, and the idol of Americans and of British regulars alike.

This year the campaign took place not in August but in July. By the middle of June it was known that Abercromby was coming. Even then Montcalm and his regulars were ready, but nothing else was. Everyone knew that Ticonderoga was the key to the south of Canada; yet the fort was not ready, though the Canadian engineers had been tinkering at it for two whole summers. These engineers were, in fact, friends of Bigot, and had found that they could make money by spinning the work out as long as possible, charging for good material and putting in bad, and letting the gang plunder the stores on the way to the fort. Montcalm had arranged everything in 1756, and there was no good reason why Ticonderoga should not have been in perfect order in 1758, when the fate of Canada was hanging on its strength. But it was not. It had not even been rightly planned. The engineers were fools as well as knaves. When the proper French army engineers arrived, having been sent out at the last moment, they were horrified at the mess that had been made of the work. But it was too late then. Montcalm and Abercromby were both advancing; and Montcalm would have to make up with the lives of his men for all that the knaves and fools had done against him.

Bad as this was, there was a still worse trouble. Vaudreuil now thought he saw a chance for another raid which would please the Canadians and hurt Montcalm. So he actually took away 1,600 men in June and sent them off to the Mohawk valley, farther west, under Levis, who ought to have known better than to have allowed himself to be flattered into taking command. This came near to wrecking the whole defence. But the owls did not see, and the foxes did not care.

Meanwhile, Montcalm was hurrying his little handful of regulars to the front. He was to leave on June 24. On the night of the 23rd Vaudreuil sent a long string of foolish orders, worded in such a way by some of his foxy parasites that the credit for any victory would come to himself, while the blame for any failure would rest on Montcalm. This was more than flesh and blood could endure. Once before Montcalm had tried to open Vaudreuil's eyes to the mischief that was going on. Now he spoke out again, and proved his case so plainly that, for very shame, Vaudreuil had to change the orders. Montcalm arrived at Ticonderoga with his new engineers on the 30th. Here he found 3,000 men and one bad fort. And the British were closing in with 15,000 men and good artillery.

The two armies lay only the length of Lake George apart, a little over thirty miles; in positions the same as last year, except that Montcalm was now on the defensive with less than half as many men, and the British were on the offensive with more than twice as many. Montcalm's great object was to gain time. Every minute was precious. He sent messenger after messenger, begging Vaudreuil to hurry forward the Canadians and to call back the Mohawk valley raiding party of 1,600 men. His 3,000 harassed regulars were working almost night and day. The fort was patched up until nothing more could be done without pulling it down and building a new fort; and an entrenched camp was dug in front of it. Meanwhile Montcalm's little army, though engaged in all this work, was actually making such a show of force about the valley between the lakes that it checked the British, who now gave up their plan of seizing a forward position in the valley as a cover for the advance of the main body later on. Montcalm, with 3,000 toil-worn soldiers, had out-generalled Abercromby and Howe with 15,000 fresh ones. He had also gained four priceless days.

But on July 5 the British advanced in force. It had been a great sight the year before, when Montcalm had gone south along Lake George with 5,000 men; but how much more magnificent now, when Abercromby came north with 15,00 men, all eager for this Armageddon of the West. Perhaps there never has been any other occasion on which the pride and pomp of glorious war have been set in a scene of such wonderful peace and beauty. The midsummer day was perfectly calm. Not a cloud was in the sky. The lovely lake shone like a burnished mirror. The forest-clad mountains never looked greener or cooler; nor did their few bare crags or pinnacles ever stand out more clearly against the endless blue sky than when those thousand boats rowed on to what 15,000 men thought certain victory.

The procession of boats was wide enough to stretch from shore to shore; yet it was much longer than its width. On each side went the Americans, 9,000 men in blue and buff. In the centre came 6,000 British regulars in scarlet and gold, among them a thousand kilted Highlanders of the splendid 'Black Watch,' led by their major, Duncan Campbell of Inverawe, whose weird had told him a year before that he should fight and fall at a place with what was then to him an unknown name—Ticonderoga.[1] The larger boats were in the rear, lashed together, two by two, with platforms laid across them for artillery.

And so the brave array advanced. The colours fluttered gallantly with the motion of the boats. The thousands of brilliant scarlet uniforms showed gaily between the masses of more sober blue. The drums were beating, the bugles blowing, the bagpipes screaming defiance to the foe; and every echo in the surrounding hills was roused to send its own defiance back.

The British halted for the night a few miles short of the north end of the lake. Next morning; the 6th, they set out again in time to land about noon within four miles of Ticonderoga in a straight line. There were two routes by which an army could march from Lake George to Lake Champlain. The first, the short way, was to go eastward across the four-mile valley. The second was twice as far, north and then east, all the way round through the woods. Since the valley road led to a bridge which Montcalm had blown up, Lord Howe went round

---

1. *The Black Watch at Ticonderoga* by Frederick B. Richards and *Montcalm at the Battle of Carillon (Ticonderoga) (July 8th, 1758* by Maurice Sautai, also published by Leonaur.

through the woods with a party of rangers to see if that way would do. While he was pushing ahead the French reconnoitring party, which, from under cover, had been following the British movements the day before, was trying to find its own way back to Montcalm through the same woods. Its Indian guides had run away in the night, scared out of their wits by the size of the British army. It was soon lost and, circling round, came between Howe and Abercromby. Suddenly the rangers and the French met in the dense forest. 'Who goes there?' shouted a Frenchman. 'Friends!' answered a British soldier in perfect French. But the uniforms told another tale and both sides fired. The French were soon overpowered by numbers, and the fifty or so survivors were glad to scurry off into the bush. But they had dealt one mortal blow. Lord Howe had fallen, and, with him, the head and heart of the whole British force.

Abercromby, a helpless leader, pottered about all the next day, not knowing what to do. Meanwhile Montcalm kept his men hard at work, and by night he was ready and hopeful. He had just written to his friend Doreil, the commissary of war at Quebec: 'We have only eight days' provisions. I have no Canadians and no Indians. The British have a very strong army. But I do not despair. My soldiers are good. From the movements of the British I can see they are in doubt. If they are slow enough to let me entrench the heights of Ticonderoga, I shall beat them.' He had ended his dispatch to Vaudreuil with similar words: 'If they only let me entrench the heights I shall beat them.' And now, on the night of the 7th, he actually was holding the heights with his 3,000 French regulars against the total British force of 15,000. Could he win on the 8th?

Late in the evening 300 regulars arrived under an excellent officer, Pouchot. At five the next morning, the fateful July 8, Levis came in with 100 more. These were all, except 400 Canadians who arrived in driblets, some while the battle was actually going on. Vaudreuil had changed his mind again, and had decided to recall the Mohawk valley raiders. But too late. Levis, Pouchot, and the Canadians had managed to get through only after a terrible forced march, spurred on by the hope of reaching their beloved Montcalm in time. The other men from the raid, and five times as many more from Canada, came in afterwards. But again too late.

The odds in numbers were four to one against Montcalm. Even in the matter of position he was anything but safe. The British could have forced him out of it by taking 10,000 men through the woods towards

Crown Point, to cut off his retreat to the north, while leaving 5,000 in front of him to protect their march and harass his own embarkation. And even if they had chosen to attack him where he was they could have used their cannon with great effect from Rattlesnake Hill, overlooking his left flank, only a mile away, or from the bush straight in front of him, at much less than half that distance, or from both places together. Always on the alert he was ready for anything, retreat included, though he preferred fighting where he was, especially if the British were foolish enough to attack without their guns—the very thing they seemed about to do. After Howe's death they made mistakes that worked both ways against them. They waited long enough to let Montcalm get ready to meet their infantry; but not long enough to get their guns ready to meet him.

Now, too, blundering Abercromby believed a stupid engineer who said the trenches could be rushed with the bayonet—precisely what could not be done. The peninsula of Ticonderoga was strong towards Lake Champlain, the narrows of which it entirely commanded. But, against infantry, it was even stronger towards the land, where trenches had been dug. The peninsula was almost a square. It jutted out into the lake about three-quarters of a mile, and its neck was of nearly the same width. Facing landward, the direction from which the British came, the left half of the peninsula was high, the right low. Montcalm entrenched the left half and put his French regulars there. He made a small trench in the middle of the right half for the Canadian regulars and militia, and cut down the trees everywhere, all round. The position of the Canadians was not strong in itself; but if the British rushed it they would be taken in flank by the French and in front by the fort, which was half a mile in rear of the trenches and could fire in any direction; while if they turned to rush the French right, they would have to charge uphill with the fire of the fort on their left.

Montcalm's men were already at work at five o'clock in the morning of the 8th when Levis marched in; and they went on working like ants till the battle began, though all day the heat was terrific. Some of the trees cut down were piled up like the wall of a log-cabin, only not straight but zigzag, like a 'snake' fence, so that the enemy should be caught between two fires at every angle. This zigzag wooden wall was, of course, well loopholed. In front of it was its zigzag ditch; and in front of the ditch were fallen trees, with their branches carefully trimmed and sharpened, and pointing outwards against the enemy. To make sure that his men should know their places in battle Montcalm held a short rehearsal. Then all fell to work again with shovel, pick, and axe.

Presently five hundred British Indians under Sir William Johnson appeared on Rattlesnake Hill and began to amuse themselves by firing off their muskets, which, of course, were perfectly useless at a distance of a mile. In the meantime Abercromby had drawn back his men from the woods and had made up his mind to take the short cut through the valley and rebuild the bridge which Montcalm had destroyed. This took up the whole morning; and it was not till noon that the British advance guard began to drive in the French outposts.

A few shots were heard. The outposts came back to the trenches. French officers on the look-out spied the blue rangers coming towards the far side of the clearings and spreading out cautiously to right and left. Then, in the centre, a mass of moving red and the fitful glitter of steel told Montcalm that his supreme moment had come at last. He raised his hand above his head. An officer, posted in the rear, made a signal to the fort half a mile farther back. A single cannon fired one shot; and every soldier laid down his tools and took up his musket. In five minutes a line three-deep had been formed behind the zigzag stockade, which looked almost like the front half of a square.

The face towards the enemy was about five hundred yards long. The left face was about two hundred yards, and the right, overlooking the low ground, ran back quite three hundred. Levis had charge of the right, Bourlamaque of the left. Montcalm himself took the centre, straight in the enemy's way. As he looked round, for the last time, and saw how steadily that long, white, three-deep, zigzag line was standing at its post of danger, with the blue Royal Roussillon in the middle, and the grenadiers drawn up in handy bodies just behind, ready to rush to the first weak spot, he thrilled with the pride of the soldier born who has an army fit to follow him.

All round the far side of the clearing the blue rangers were running, stooping, slinking forward, and increasing in numbers every second. In a few minutes not a stump near the edge of the bush but had a muzzle pointing out from beside it. Soon not one but four great, solid masses of redcoats were showing through the trees, less than a quarter of a mile away. Presently they all formed up correctly, and stood quite still for an anxious minute or two. Then, as if each red column was a single being, with heart and nerves of its own, the whole four stirred with that short, tense quiver which runs through every mass of men when they prepare to meet death face to face. Behind the loopholed wall there was a murmur from three thousand lips—'Here they come!'—and the answering quiver ran through the zigzag, white ranks of the French, Montcalm's officers immediately repeated his last caution: 'Steady, boys. Don't fire till the red-coats reach the stakes and you get the word!'

At the edge of the trees the British officers were also reminding their men about the orders. 'Remember: no firing at all; nothing but the bayonet; and follow the officers in!' *Quick-March!* and the four dense columns came out of the wood, drew clear of it altogether, and advanced with steady tramp, their muskets at the shoulder and their bayonets gleaming with a deadly sheen under the fierce, hot, noonday sun. On they came, four magnificent processions, full of the pride of arms and the firm hope of glorious victory. Three of them were uniform masses of ordinary redcoats. But the fourth, making straight for Montcalm himself, was half grenadiers, huge men with high-pointed hats, and half Highlanders, with swinging kilts and dancing plumes. The march was a short one; but it seemed long, for at every step the suspense became greater and greater. At last the leading officers suddenly waved their swords, the bugles rang out the *Charge!* and then, as if the four eager columns had been slipped from one single leash together, they dashed at the trees with an exultant roar that echoed round the hills like thunder.

Montcalm gripped his sword, and every French finger tightened on the trigger. His colonels watched him eagerly. Up went his sword and up went theirs. *Ready!—Present!—Fire!!* and a terrific, double-shotted, point-blank volley crashed out of that zigzag wall and simply swept away the heads of the charging columns. But the men in front were no sooner mown down than the next behind them swarmed forward. Again the French fired, again the leading British fell, and again more British rushed forward. The British sharp-shooters now spread out in swarms on the flanks of the columns and fired back, as did the first ranks of the columns themselves. But they had much the worse of this kind of fighting. Again the columns surged forward, broke up as they reached the trees, and were shot down as they struggled madly among the sharpened branches.

Montcalm had given orders that each man was to fire for himself, whenever he could get a good shot at an enemy; and that the officers were only to look after the powder and shot, see that none was wasted, and keep their men steady in line. His own work was to watch the whole fight and send parties of grenadiers from his reserve to any

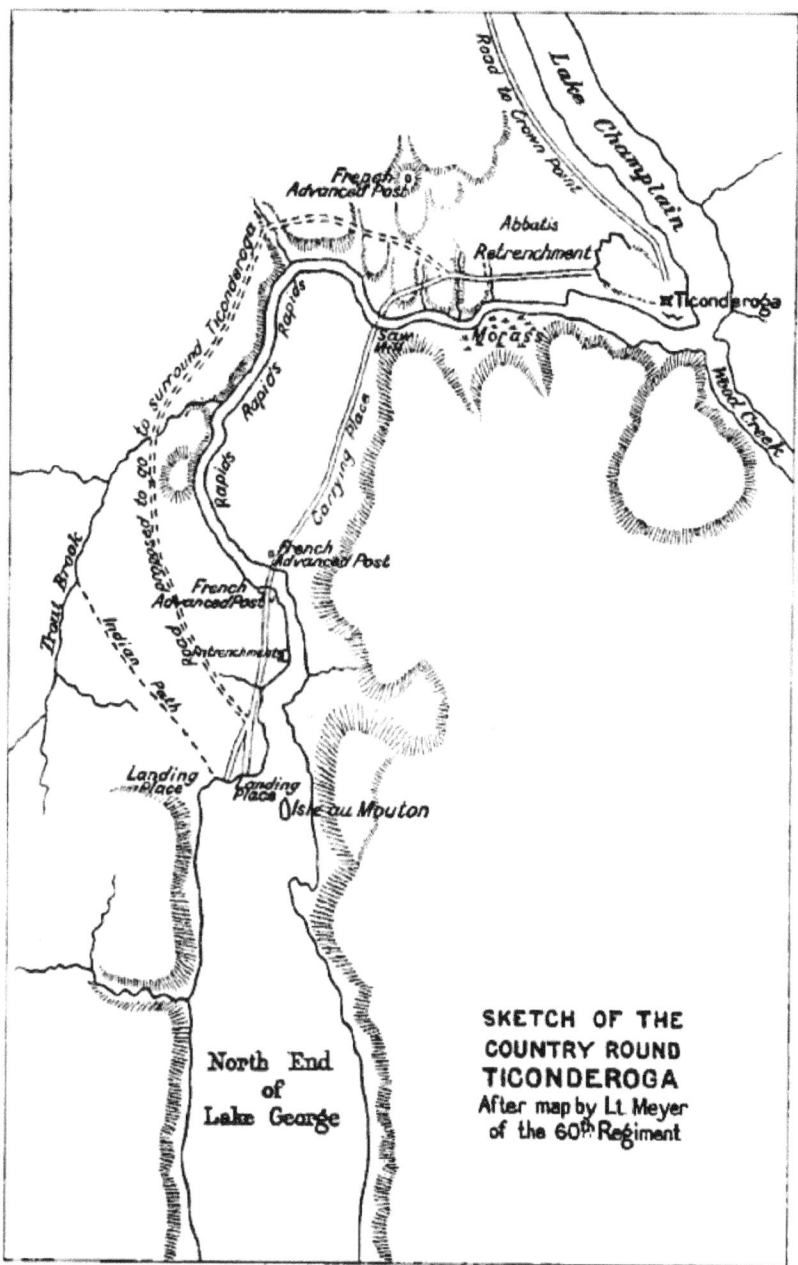

Lake Champlain

Road to Crown Point

French Advanced Post

Abbatis Retrenchment

Ticonderoga

to surround Ticonderoga

Rapid's Rapids

Rapids

Saw Mill

Morass

Wood Creek

Carrying Place

French Advanced Post

to go to prevent the Retreat

French Advanced Post

Trout Brook

Indian Path

Retrenchment

Landing Place

Landing Place

I'sle au Mouton

North End
of
Lake George

SKETCH OF THE
COUNTRY ROUND
TICONDEROGA
After map by Lt. Meyer
of the 60ᵗʰ Regiment

point where the enemy seemed likely to break in. But the defence weakened only in a single place, where the regiment of Berry, which had a good many recruits, wavered and began to sway back from its loopholes. Its officers, however, were among their men in a moment, and had put them into their places again before the grenadiers whom Montcalm sent running down could reach them.

Again and again the British sharpshooters repeated their fire; again and again the heads of the columns were renewed by the men behind, as those in front were mown down by the French. At last, but slowly, sullenly, and turning to have shot after shot at that stubborn defence of Montcalm's, the redcoats gave way and retreated, leaving hundreds of killed and wounded behind them. Montcalm was sure now that all was going well. He had kept several officers moving about the line, and their reports were all of the same kind—'men steady, firing well, no waste of ammunition, not many killed and wounded, all able to hold their own.'

Here and there a cartridge or grenade had set the wooden walls alight. But men were ready with water; and even when the flames caught on the side towards the enemy there was no lack of volunteers to jump down and put them out. The fort, half a mile in rear and overlooking the whole scene, did good work with its guns. Once it stopped an attack on the extreme left by a flotilla of barges which came out of the mouth of the river running through the four-mile valley between the lakes. Two barges were sent to the bottom. Several others were well peppered by the French reserves, who ran down to the bank of the river; and the rest turned round and rowed back as hard as they could.

In all this heat of action Vaudreuil was not forgotten; but he would not have felt flattered by what the soldiers said. All knew how slow he had been about sending the Canadians, 3,000 of whom were already long overdue. 'Bah!' they said during the first lull in the battle; 'the governor has sold the colony; but we won't let him deliver the goods! God save the King and Montcalm!'

This first lull was not for long. On came the four red columns again, just as stubborn as before. Again they charged. Again they split up in front as they reached the fatal trees. Again they were shot down. Again rank after rank replaced the one that fell before it. Again the sharpshooters stood up to that death-dealing loopholedwall. And again the British retired slowly and sullenly, leaving behind them four larger heaps of killed and wounded.

A strange mistake occurred on both sides. Whenever the French soldiers shouted 'God save the King and Montcalm,' the ensigns carrying the colours of the regiment of Guienne waved them high in the air. The flags were almost white, and some of the British mistook them for a sign of surrender. Calling out 'Quarter, Quarter!' the redcoats held their muskets above their heads and ran in towards the wall. The French then thought it was the British who wished to surrender, and called out 'Ground Arms!' But Pouchot, the officer who had marched night and day from the Mohawk valley to join Montcalm, seeing what he thought a serious danger that the British would break through, called out 'Fire!' and his men, most of them leaning over the top of the wall, poured in a volley that cut down more than a hundred of the British.

The Canadians in the separate trench on the low ground, at the extreme right, were not closely engaged at all. They and the American rangers took pot-shots at each other without doing much harm on either side. In the middle of the battle the Canadians were joined by 250 of their friends, just come in from Lake Champlain. But even with this reinforcement they made only a very feeble attack on the exposed left flank of the British column nearest to them on the higher ground, in spite of the fact that this column was engaged in a keen fight with the French in its front, and was getting much the worse of it. When Levis sent two French officers down to lead an attack on the British column the Canadian officers joined it at once. But the mass of the men hung back. They were raiders and bush-fighters. They had no bayonets. Above all, they did not intend to come to close quarters if they could help it. Ticonderoga was no attack by men from the British colonies and no French-Canadian defence and victory. It was a stand-up fight between the French and the British regulars, who settled it between themselves alone.

About five o'clock the two left columns of the British joined forces to make a supreme effort. They were led by the Highlanders, who charged with the utmost fury, while the two right columns made an equally brave attack elsewhere. The front ranks were shot down as before. But the men in rear rushed forward so fast—every fallen man seeming to make ten more spring over his body—that Montcalm was alarmed, and himself pressed down at the head of his grenadiers to the point where the fight was hottest. At the same time Levis, finding his own front clear of the old fourth column, brought over the regiment of La Reine and posted it in rear of the men who most needed its support. These two reinforcements turned the scale of victory, and the charge failed.

Abercromby, unlike Montcalm, never exposed himself on the field at all. But, for the second time, he sent word that the trenches must be taken with the bayonet. The response was another attack. But the men were tired out by the sweltering heat and a whole afternoon of desperate fighting. They advanced, fired, had their front ranks shot down again; and once more retired in sullen silence. The last British attack had failed. Their sharp-shooters and the American rangers covered the retreat. Montcalm had won the day, the most glorious that French arms had seen in the whole of their long American career.

The British had lost 2,000 men, nearly all regulars. But they still had 4,000 regulars left, more than Montcalm's entire command could muster now. He went into action with 3,500 French regulars, 150 Canadian regulars, 250 Canadian militia, and 15 Indians: a total of 3,915. At four o'clock 250 more Canadians arrived. But as his loss was 400 killed and wounded, nearly all French regulars, he had not 4,000 fit for action, of all kinds together, at any one time; and he ended the day with only 3,765. On the other hand, Abercromby still had nearly all his 9,000 militia, besides 500 Indians; who, though worthless in the battle, were dangerous in the bush. Under these conditions it would have been sheer madness for Montcalm to have followed the British into their own country, especially as he lacked food almost more than he lacked men.

The losses of the different kinds of troops on both sides show us by whom most of the fighting was done. The Indians had no losses, either from among the 15 French or the 500 British. The Canadians and the American militia each lost about one man in every twenty-seven. The French regulars, fighting behind entrenchments and under a really great general; lost in proportion about three times as many as these others did, or one man in every nine. The British regulars, fighting in the open against entrenchments and under a blundering commander, lost nearly one man in every three.

Abercromby, having been pig-headed in his advance, now became chicken-hearted in his retreat. He was in no danger. Yet he ran like a hare. Had it not been for his steady regulars and some old hands among the rangers his return would have become a perfect rout. Pitt soon got rid of him; and he retired into private life with the well-earned nickname of 'Mrs. Nabby-Cromby.'

Montcalm was a devout man. He felt that the issue of the day had been the result of an appeal to the God of Battles; and he set up a cross on the ground he had won, with a Latin inscription that shows both his modesty and his scholarship:

Quid dux? Quid miles? Quid strata ingentia ligna?
En signum! En victor! Deus hic, Deus ipse, triumphat!

General, soldier, and ramparts are as naught!
Behold the conquering Cross! 'Tis God the triumph wrought!

But the glorious joy of victory did not last long. Vaudreuil claimed most of the credit for himself and the Canadians. He wrote lying dispatches to France and senseless orders to Montcalm. Now that reinforcements were worse than useless, because they ate up the food and could not attack the enemy, he kept on sending them every day. Montcalm was stung to the quick by the letters he received. After getting three foolish orders to march into the British colonies he wrote back sharply:

'I think it very strange that you find yourself, at a distance of a hundred and fifty miles, so well able to make war in a country you have never seen!'

Nor was this all. Vaudreuil had also sent Indians, of course after the need for them had passed. They were idle and a perfect nuisance to the French. They began stealing the hospital stores and all the strong drink they could lay hands on. Montcalm checked them sharply. Then they complained to Vaudreuil, and Vaudreuil reproached Montcalm.

It was the same wretched story over and over again: the owls and foxes in the rear thwarting, spiting and robbing the lions at the front. Montcalm was more sick at heart than ever. He saw that anything he could say or do was of little use; and he again asked to be recalled. But he soon heard news which made him change his mind, no matter what the cost to his feelings. The east and the west had both fallen into British hands. Louisbourg and the Ohio were taken. Only Canada itself remained; and, even now, Pitt was planning to send against it overpowering forces both by sea and land. Montcalm would not, could not, leave the ruined colony he had fought for so long against such fearful odds. In the desperate hope of saving it from impending doom, he decided to stay to the end.

CHAPTER 6

Quebec 1759

Having decided to stay in Canada Montcalm did all he could to come to terms with Vaudreuil, so that the French might meet with a united front the terrible dangers of the next campaign. He spoke straight out in a letter written to Vaudreuil on August 2, less than a month after his victory at Ticonderoga:

> I think the real trouble lies with the people who compose your letters, and with the mischief-makers who are trying to set you against me. You may be sure that none of the things which are being done against me will ever lessen my zeal for the good of the country or my respect towards you, the governor. Why not change your secretary's style? Why not give me more of your confidence? I take the liberty of saying that the king's service would gain by it, and we should no longer appear so disunited that even the British know all about it. I enclose a newspaper printed in New York which mentions it. False reports are made to you. Efforts are made to embitter you against me. I think you need not suspect my military conduct, when I am really doing all I can. After my three years of command under your orders what need is there for your secretary to tell me about the smallest trifles and give me petty orders that I should myself blush to give to a junior captain?

When Montcalm wrote this he had not yet heard the bad news from Louisbourg and the Ohio, and he was still anxious to be recalled to France. Vaudreuil, of course, was delighted at the prospect of getting rid of him. He wrote home to France,:

> I beseech you to ask the king to recall the Marquis of Mont-

calm. He desires it himself. The king has confided Canada to my own care, and I cannot help thinking that it would be a very bad thing for the marquis to remain here any longer!

There spoke the owl. And here the lion, when the bad news came:

I had asked for my recall after Ticonderoga. But since the affairs of Canada are getting worse, it is my duty to help in setting them right again, or at least to stave off ruin so long as I can.

Vaudreuil and Montcalm met and talked matters over. Even the governor began to see that the end was near, unless France should send out help in the spring of 1759. He was so scared at the idea of losing his governorship in such an event that he actually agreed with Montcalm to send two honest and capable men to France to tell the king and his ministers the truth. Two officers, Bougainville and Doreil, were chosen. They sailed in November with letters from both Montcalm and Vaudreuil. Nothing could have been better or truer than the letters Vaudreuil gave them to present at court. 'Colonel Bougainville is, in all respects, better fitted than anybody else to inform you of the state of the colony. I have given him my orders, and you can trust entirely in everything he tells you.' 'M. Doreil, the commissary of war, may be entirely trusted. Everybody likes him here.' But, by the same ship, the same Vaudreuil wrote a secret letter against these officers and against Montcalm.

In order to condescend to the Marquis of Montcalm and do all I can to keep on good terms with him I have given letters to Colonel Bougainville and M. Doreil. But I must tell you that they do not really know Canada well, and I warn you that they are nothing but creatures of the Marquis of Montcalm.

The winter of 1758-59 was like the two before it, only very much worse. The three might be described, in so many words, as bad, worse, and worst of all. Doreil had seen the stores and provisions of the army plundered by the Bigot gang, the soldiers half starved, the supposed presents for the Indians sold to them at the highest possible price, and the forts badly built of bad materials by bad engineers, who made a Bigot-gang profit out of their work. A report was also going home from a French inspector who had been sent out to see why the cost of government had been rising by leaps and bounds. Things were cheap in those days, and money was scarce and went a long way. When this was the case the whole public expense of Canada for a year should not have been more than one million dollars. But in Montcalm's first year it had already passed two millions. In his second it had passed four. And now, in his third, it was getting very near to eight.

Where did the money go? Just where all public money always goes when parasites govern a country. The inspector found out that many items of cost for supplies to the different posts had a cipher added to them. The officials told him why: 'We have to do it because the price of living has gone up ten times over.' But how did such an increase come about? The goods were sold from favourite to favourite, each man getting his wholly illegal profit, till the limit was reached beyond which Bigot thought it would not be safe to go. By means of false accounts, by lying reports and by the aid of accomplices in France who stopped letters from Montcalm and other honest men, the game went on for two years. Now it was found out.

But the gang was still too strong in Canada to be broken up. In France it was growing weak. Another couple of years and all its members would have been turned out by the home government. They knew this; and, seeing that their end was coming in one way or another, they thought a British conquest could not be much worse than a French prison; indeed, it might be better, for a complete and general ruin might destroy proof of their own guilt. The lions would die fighting—and a good thing too! But the owls and foxes might escape with the spoils. 'What a country, where knaves grow rich and honest men are ruined!'

Montcalm wrote home to his family by every ship. He might not have long to do so. Just after Ticonderoga he wrote to his wife:

Thank God! it is all over now until the beginning of May. We shall have desperate work in the next campaign. The enemy will have 50,000 men in the field, all together; and we, how many? I dare not tell it. *Adieu*, my heart, I long for peace and you. When shall I see my Candiac again?'

On November 21, 1758, the last ship left for France. He wrote to his old mother, to whom he had always told the story of his wars, from the time when, thirty-one years before, as a stripling of fifteen, he had joined his father's regiment in the very year that Wolfe was born:

You will be glad to hear from me up to the last moment and know, for the hundredth time, that I am always thinking of you all at home, in spite of the fate of New France and my duty with the army and the state. We did our best these last three years; and so, God helping us, we shall in 1759—unless you can make a peace for us in Europe.

The wretched winter dragged on. The French were on half rations, the Canadians worse off still. In January Montcalm wrote in his diary: 'terrible distress round Quebec.' Then, the same day: 'balls, amusements, picnics, and tremendous gambling.' Another entry: 'in spite of the distress and impending ruin of the colony pleasure parties are going on the whole time.' He himself had only plain fare—horse-flesh and the soldier's half ration of bread—on his table. No wonder the vampires hated him!

May came; but not a word from France. For eight whole months no French ship had been able to cross the sea, to bring aid for the needy colony. Day by day the half-starved people scanned the St Lawrence for sight of a sail. At last, on the 10th, they had their reward. A French ship arrived; more ships followed; and by the 20th there were twenty-three in the harbour, all laden with provisions, stores, and men. The help was inadequate. There were only 326 soldiers for Montcalm on board, and there were not enough provisions to keep the soldiers and people on full rations through the summer, even with the help of what crops might be harvested while the farmers remained under arms. But Montcalm made the best of it: 'a little is precious to those who have nothing.'

Bougainville brought out plenty of promotions and honours for the victory at Ticonderoga. Montcalm was made lieutenant-general of the king in Canada. Bougainville told him his name was known all over France; 'even the children use it in their games.' Old Marshal Belle Isle, a gallant veteran, now at the head of the French army, and a great admirer of Montcalm, had sent out the king's last orders:

No matter how small the space may be that you can retain, you must somehow keep a foothold in America; for, if we once lose the whole country, we shall never get it back again. The king counts upon your zeal, your courage, and your firmness to spare no pains and no exertion. You must hold out to the very last, whatever happens. I have answered for you to the king.

Montcalm replied: 'I shall do everything to maintain a foothold in New France, or die in its defence'; and he kept his word.

There was both joy and sorrow in the news from Candiac. His eldest daughter was happily married. His eldest son was no less happily

151

engaged. But, at the last minute, Bougainville had heard that another daughter had died suddenly; he did not know which one. 'It must be poor Mirete,' said Montcalm, 'I love her so much.' His last letters home show with what a brave despair he faced the coming campaign.

> Can we hope for another miracle to save us? God's will be done! I await news from France with impatience and dread. We had none for eight months, and who knows if we shall have any more this year. How dearly I have to pay for the dismal privilege of figuring in the Gazette. I would give up all my honours to see you again. But the king must be obeyed. *Adieu*, my heart, I believe I love you more than ever!

Bougainville had also brought out the news that Pitt was sending enormous forces to conquer Canada for good and all. One army was to attack the last French posts on the Lakes. Another was to come up Lake Champlain and take Montreal. A combined fleet and army, under Saunders and Wolfe, was to undertake the most difficult task and to besiege Quebec. There was no time to lose. Even Vaudreuil saw that. Pouchot was left at Niagara with 1,000 men. De la Corne had another 1,000 on the shores of Lake Ontario. Bourlamaque held Lake Champlain with 3,000. But the key of all Canada was Quebec; and so every man who could be spared was brought down to defend it. Saunders and Wolfe had 27,000 men of all kinds, 9,000 soldiers and 18,000 sailors, mostly man-of-war's-men. The total number which the French could collect to meet them was 17,000. Of these 17,000 only 4,000 were French regulars. There were over 1,000 Canadian regulars; less than 2,000 sailors, very few of whom were man-of-war's-men; about 10,000 Canadian militia, and a few hundred Indians. The militia included old men and young boys, any one, in fact, who could fire off a musket. The grand totals, all over the seat of war, were 44,000 British against 22,000 French.

Having done all he could for Niagara, Ontario, and Lake Champlain, Montcalm hurried down to Quebec on May 22. Vaudreuil followed on the 23rd. On the same day the advance guard of the British fleet arrived at Bic on the lower St Lawrence. From that time forward New France was sealed up as completely as if it had shrunk to a single fort. Nothing came in and nothing went out. The strangling coils of British sea-power were all round it. But still Montcalm stood defiantly at bay. 'You must maintain your foothold to the very last.'—'I shall do it or die.'

His plan was to keep the British at arm's length as long as possible. The passage known as the 'Traverse' from the north channel to the south, at the lower end of the Island of Orleans, was a good place to begin. Strong batteries there might perhaps sink enough of the fleet to block the way for the rest. These Montcalm was eager to build, but Vaudreuil was not. Had not Vaudreuil's Canadian pilots prophesied that no British fleet could possibly ascend the river in safety, even without any batteries to hinder it? And was not Vaudreuil so sure of this himself that he had never had the Traverse properly sounded at all? He would allow no more than a couple of useless batteries, which the first British men-of-war soon put to silence. The famous Captain Cook, who was sailing master of a frigate on this expedition, made the necessary soundings in three days; and the fleet of forty warships and a hundred transports went through without a scratch.

Vaudreuil's second chance was with seven fireships, which, having been fitted out by the Bigot gang at ten times the proper cost, were commanded by a favoured braggart called Delouche. The night after the British fleet had arrived in the Orleans Channel, the whole French camp turned out to watch what it was hoped would be a dramatic and effective attack on the mass of shipping which lay at anchor near the head of the island. The fireships were sent down with the ebb-tide, straight for the crowded British fleet. But Delouche lost his nerve, fired his ship too soon, jumped into a boat and rowed away. Five of the others did the same. The seventh was a hero, Dubois de la Milletiere, who stuck to his post, but was burned to death there in a vain effort to get among the enemy. Had the six others waited longer the whole of the seven French crews might have escaped together and some damage might have been done to the British. As it was there was nothing but splendid fireworks for both sides. The best man on the French side was killed for nothing; no harm was done to the British; and for equipping the fireships the Bigot gang put another hundred thousand stolen dollars into their thievish pockets. 'What a country, where knaves grow rich and honest men are ruined!'

Vaudreuil's third chance was to defend the shore opposite Quebec, Point Levis, which Montcalm wished to hold as long as possible. If the French held it the British fleet could not go past Quebec, between two fires, and Wolfe could not bombard the town from the opposite heights. But, early in July, Vaudreuil withdrew the French troops from Point Levis, and Wolfe at once occupied the shore and began to build his batteries. As soon as the British had made themselves secure

Vaudreuil thought it time to turn them out. But he sent only 1,500 men; and so many of these were boys and youths at school and college that the French troops dubbed them 'The Royal Syntax.' These precious 1,500 went up the north shore, crossed over after dark, and started to march, in two separate columns, down the south shore towards Levis. Presently the first column heard a noise in the woods and ran back to join the second. But the second, seeing what it mistook for the enemy, fired into the first and ran for dear life. Then the first, making a similar mistake, blazed into the second, and, charmed with its easy victory, started hotfoot in pursuit. After shooting at each other a little more, just to make sure, the two lost columns joined together again and beat a hasty retreat.

With the opposite shore lost Montcalm had now no means of keeping Wolfe at any distance. But Montcalm had chosen his position with skill, and it was so strong by nature that it might yet be held till the autumn, if only he was allowed to defend it in his own way. His left was protected by the Montmorency River, narrow, but deep and rapid, with only two fords, one in thick bush, where the British regulars would have least chance, and another at the mouth, directly under the fire of the French left. His centre was the six miles of ground stretching towards Quebec between the Montmorency and the little river St Charles. Here the bulk of his army was strongly entrenched, mostly on rising ground, just beyond the shore of the great basin of the St Lawrence, the wide oozy tidal flats of which the British would have to cross if they tried to attack him in front. His right was Quebec itself and the heights of the north shore above.

Wolfe pitched his camp on the far side of the cliffs near the Falls of Montmorency; and one day tried to cross the upper fords, four miles above the falls, to attack Montcalm in the rear. But Montcalm was ready for him in the bush and beat him back.

The next British move was against the left of Montcalm's entrenchments. On July 31 Wolfe's army was busy at an early hour; and all along the French front men-of-war were under way with their decks cleared for action. At ten o'clock, when the tide was high, two small armed ships were run aground opposite the French redoubt on the beach a mile from the falls; and they, the men-of-war, and Wolfe's batteries beyond the falls, all began to fire on the redoubt and the trenches behind it. Montcalm fired back so hard at the two armed ships that the British had to leave them. Then he gave orders for his army to be ready to come at a moment's notice, but to keep away

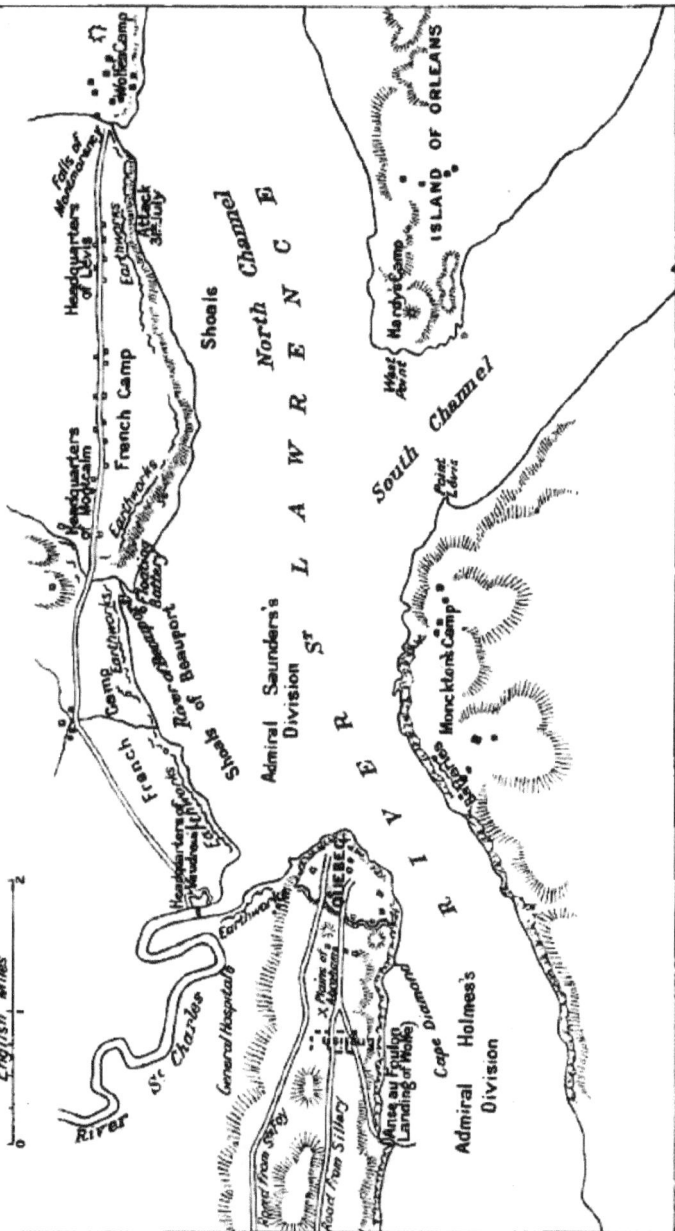

SIEGE OF QUEBEC
1759

English Miles

River

St Charles

General Hospital

Quebec

Earthworks

Plains of Abraham

Anse au Foulon
(Landing of Wolfe)

Cape Diamond

Road from Sillery

Road from Sillery

Admiral Holmes's Division

Headquarters of Vaudreuil
Earthworks

French entrenchments

French Camp

Earthworks

River Beauport

Shoals of Beauport

Headquarters of Montcalm

French Camp

Earthworks

Shoals

ST LAWRENCE

North Channel

RIVER

Admiral Saunders's Division

South Channel

West Point

Point Levis

Monckton's Camp

Headquarters of Lévis
Redoubt
Earthworks
Falls of Montmorency

Wolfe's Camp

Hardy's Camp

ISLAND OF ORLEANS

Bartholomew, Edin.

from the threatened point for the present. By this means, and from the fact that his trenches had been very cleverly made by his own French engineers, he lost very few men, even though the British kept up a furious fire.

The British kept cannonading all day. By four o'clock one British brigade was trying to land beside the two stranded armed ships, and the two other brigades were seen to be ready to join it from their camp at Montmorency. The redcoats had plenty of trouble in landing; and it was not till six that their grenadiers, a thousand strong, were forming up to lead the attack. Suddenly there was an outburst of cheering from the British sailors. The grenadiers mistook this for the commencement of the attack. They broke their ranks and dashed madly at the redoubt. The garrison at once left it and ran back, up the hill, into the trenches. The grenadiers climbed into it, pell-mell; but, as it was open towards its rear, it gave them no cover from the terrific fire that the French, on Montcalm's signal, now poured into them. Again they made a mad charge, this time straight at the trenches. Montcalm had called in every man there was room for, and such a storm of bullets, grape-shot, cannon-balls, and shells now belched forth that even British grenadiers could not face it. A thunderstorm burst, with a deluge of rain; and, amid the continued roar of nature's and man's artillery, half the grenadiers were seen retreating, while half remained dead or wounded on the field.

The two redcoat brigades from Montmorency had now joined the remnant of the first, which had had such a rough experience. Montcalm kept his men well in hand to meet this more formidable attack. But Wolfe had had enough. The first brigade went back to its boats. The second and third brigades marched back to Montmorency along the beach in perfect order, the men waving their hats in defiance at the French, who jumped up on top of their earthworks and waved defiance back. Before retiring the British set fire to the two stranded ships. The day had been as disastrous for Wolfe as glorious for Montcalm.

August was a hard month for both armies. Montcalm had just won his fourth victory over the British; and he would have saved Canada once more if only he could keep Wolfe out of Quebec till October. Wolfe was ill, weak, disappointed, defeated. But his army was at least perfectly safe from attack. With a powerful fleet to aid him Wolfe was never in any danger in the positions he occupied. His army was always well provisioned; even luxuries could be bought in the British camp.

The fleet patrolled the whole course of the St Lawrence; convoys of provision ships kept coming up throughout the siege, and Montcalm had no means of stopping a single vessel.

Montcalm could not stop the ships; but the ships could stop him. He was completely cut off from the rest of the world, except from the country above Quebec; and now that was being menaced too. The St Lawrence between Quebec and Montreal was the only link connecting the different parts of New France, and the only way by which Quebec could be provisioned. The course of the campaign could not have been foretold; and Montcalm had to keep provisions in several places along the river above Quebec, in case he had to retreat. It would have been foolish to put all the food into Quebec, as he would not be able to take enough away with him, should he be obliged to leave for Montreal or perhaps for the Great Lakes, or even for a last desperate stand among the swamps of New Orleans. 'You must keep a foothold in America.'—'I shall do everything to keep it, or die.' Quebec was the best of all footholds. But if not Quebec, then some other place not so good: Montreal; an outpost on the Great Lakes; a camp beyond the Mississippi; or even one beside the Gulf of Mexico.

So, for every reason, Montcalm was quite as anxious about the St Lawrence above Quebec as he was about Quebec itself. Ever since July 18 Admiral Saunders had been sending more and more ships up the river, under cover of the fire from the Levis batteries. In August things had grown worse for Montcalm. Admiral Holmes commanded a strong squadron in the river above Quebec. Under his convoy one of Wolfe's brigades landed at Deschambault, forty miles above Quebec, and burnt a magazine of food and other stores. This step promised disaster for the French. Montcalm sent Bougainville up along the north shore with 1,000 men to watch the enemy and help any of the French posts there to prevent a landing. Whenever Saunders and Wolfe sent further forces in that direction Montcalm did the same. He gave Bougainville more men. He strengthened both the shore and floating batteries, and by means of mounted messengers he kept in almost hourly touch with what was going on.

The defence of the north shore above Quebec was of the last importance. The only safe way of feeding Quebec was by barges from Montreal, Sorel, and Three Rivers, which came down without any trouble to the Richelieu rapids, a swift and narrow part of the St Lawrence near Deschambault, where some small but most obstructive French frigates and the natural difficulties in the river would probably keep Holmes from going any higher. There was further safety to the French in the fact that Wolfe could not take his army to this point from Montmorency without being found out in good time to let Montcalm march up to meet him.

It was vital to Montcalm to keep the river open. It would never do to be obliged to land provisions above Deschambault and to cart them down by road. To begin with, there were not enough carts and horses, nor enough men to be spared for driving them; and, in addition, the roads were bad. Moreover, transport by land was not to be compared with transport by water; it was easier to carry a hundred tons by water than one by land. Accordingly, Quebec was fed by way of the river. The French barges would creep down, close alongshore, at night, and try to get into the Foulon, a cove less than two miles above Quebec. Here they would unload their cargoes, which were then drawn up the hill, carted across the Plains of Abraham, and down the other side, over the bridge of boats, into the French camp.

Montcalm was anxious, but not despairing. Vaudreuil was, indeed, as mischievous as ever. But now that the two enemies were facing each other, in much the same way, for weeks together, there was less mischief for him to make. He made, however, as much as he could. Everything that happened in the French camp was likely to be known next day in the British camp. Vaudreuil could not keep any news to himself. But he tried to keep news from Montcalm and to carry out thwarting plans of his own. Wolfe had no drawbacks like this. News from his camp was always stale, because the fleet was a perfect screen, and no one on the French side could tell what was going on behind it till long after the chance had gone by.

One day Captain Vauquelin, a French naval officer, offered to board a British man-of-war that was in the way of the provision boats, if Vaudreuil would let him take five hundred men and two frigates, which he would bring down the river in the night. Vauquelin was a patriot hero, who had done well at Louisbourg the year before, and who was to do well at Quebec the year after. But, of course, he was not a member of the Bigot gang. So he was set aside in favour of a parasite, who made a hopeless bungle of the whole affair.

The siege dragged on, and every day seemed to tell in favour of Montcalm, in spite of all the hardships the French were suffering. Wolfe was pounding the city into ruins from his Levis batteries; but not getting any nearer to taking it. He was also laying most of the country waste. But this was of no use either, unless the French barges on the river could be stopped altogether, and a landing in force could be made on the north shore close to Quebec.

Wolfe was right to burn the farms from which the Canadians fired at his men. Armies may always destroy whatever is used to destroy them. But one of his British regular officers was disgracefully wrong in another matter. The greatest blackguard on either side, during the whole war, was Captain Alexander Montgomery of the 43rd Regiment, brother of the general who led the American invasion of Canada in 1775 and fell defeated before Quebec. Montgomery had a fight with the villagers of St Joachim, who had very foolishly dressed up as Indians. No quarter was given while the fight lasted, as Indians never gave it themselves. But some Canadians who surrendered were afterwards butchered in cold blood, by Montgomery's own orders, and actually scalped as well.

The siege went on with move and counter-move. Both sides knew that September must be the closing month of the drama, and French hopes rose. There was bad news for them from Lake Champlain; but it might have been much worse. Amherst was advancing towards Montreal very slowly. Bourlamaque, an excellent officer, was retreating before him, but he thought that Montreal would be safe till the next year if some French reinforcements could be sent up from Quebec. Only good troops would be of any use, and Montcalm had too few of them already. But if Amherst took Montreal the line of the St Lawrence would be cut at once. So Levis was sent off with a thousand men, a fact which Wolfe knew the very day they left.

September came. The first and second days passed quietly enough. But on the third the whole scene of action was suddenly changed. From this time on, for the next ten days, Montcalm and his army were desperately trying to stave off the last and fatal move, which ended with one of the great historic battles of the world.

CHAPTER 7

The Plains of Abraham – September 13, 1759

September 3 looked like July 31 over again. One brigade of redcoats came in boats from the Point of Levy and rowed about in front of the left of Montcalm's entrenchments. The two others marched down the hill to the foot of the Falls of Montmorency. But here, instead of fording the mouth and marching along the beach, they entered boats and joined the first brigade, which was hovering in front of the French lines. Meanwhile, the main squadron of the fleet, under Saunders himself, was closing in before these same lines, with decks cleared for action. Montcalm thought that this was likely to be Wolfe's last move, and he felt sure he could beat him again. But no attack was made. As the ships closed in towards the shore the densely crowded boats suddenly turned and rowed off to the Point of Levy. Wolfe had broken camp without the loss of a single man.

Now began for Montcalm ten terrible days and nights. From the time Wolfe left Montmorency to the time he stood upon the Plains of Abraham, Montcalm had no means whatever of finding out where the bulk of the British army was or what it intended to do. Even now, Vaudreuil had not sense enough to hold his tongue, and the French plans and movements were soon known to Wolfe, especially as the Canadians were beginning to desert in large numbers. Wolfe, on the other hand, kept his own counsel; the very few deserters from the British side knew little or nothing, and the fleet became a better screen than ever. For thirty miles, from the Falls of Montmorency up to above Pointe aux Trembles, the ships kept moving up and down, threatening first one part of the north shore and then another, and screening the south altogether. Sometimes there were movements of men-of-war, sometimes of transports, sometimes of boats, sometimes of any two of these, sometimes of all three together; sometimes there were redcoats on board one, or two, or all three kinds of craft, and sometimes not. It was a dreadful puzzle for Montcalm, a puzzle made ten times worse because all the news of the British plans that could be found out was first told to Vaudreuil.

Gradually it seemed as if Wolfe was aiming at a landing somewhere on the stretch of thirteen miles of the north shore between Cap Rouge, nine miles above Quebec, and Pointe aux Trembles, twenty-two miles above. Camp gossip, the reports from Bougainville, who was still watching Holmes up the river, and whatever other news could be gathered, all seemed to point the same way. But Saunders was still opposite the Beauport entrenchments; and the British camps at the island of Orleans, the Point of Levy, and the Levis batteries still seemed to have a good many redcoats. The use of redcoats, however, made the puzzle harder than ever at this time, for Saunders had over 2,000 marines, who were dressed in red and who at a distance could not be told from Wolfe's own soldiers.

Perhaps Wolfe was only making a feint at Pointe aux Trembles, and might, after all, come down against the entrenchments if he saw that Montcalm had weakened them. Perhaps, also, he might try to land, not at either end of the French line, but somewhere in the middle, between Cap Rouge and Quebec. Nothing could be found out definitely. Certainly the British were looking for the weakest spot, wherever it was. So Montcalm did the best he could to defend nearly thirty miles of shoreline with the reduced army of 13,000 men which he now had. Sickness, desertion, losses in battle, and the reinforcements for Lake Champlain had taken away a good 4,000. Again he reinforced Bougainville, and told him to watch more carefully than ever the menaced thirteen miles between Cap Rouge and Pointe aux Trembles. He himself looked after the garrison of Quebec. He made sure that the bulk of his army was ready to defend the Beauport entrenchments as well as before, and that it was also ready at a moment's notice to march up the river. He sent a good battalion of French regulars to guard the heights between Quebec and Cap Rouge, heights so strong by nature that nobody else seemed to think they needed defending at all.

This French battalion, that of La Guienne, marched up to their new position on the 5th, and made the nine miles between Quebec and Cap Rouge safe enough against any British attack. There were already posts and batteries to cover all the points where a body of men could get up the cliffs, and the presence of a battalion reduced to nothing the real dangers in this quarter. By the 7th Vaudreuil had decided that these real dangers did not exist, that Montcalm was all wrong, especially about the Plains of Abraham, that there could be no landing of the enemy between Quebec and Cap Rouge, that there was not enough firewood there for both the Guienne battalion and the men at the posts and batteries, and that, in short, the French regulars must march back to the entrenchments. So back they came.

On the 8th and 9th the British vessels swarmed round Pointe aux Trembles. How many soldiers there were on board was more than Bougainville could tell. He knew only that a great many had been seen first from Cap Rouge, that later a great many had been seen from Pointe aux Trembles, and that every day bodies of soldiers had been landed and taken on board again at St Nicholas, on the south shore, between the two positions of Cap Rouge and Pointe aux Trembles. The British plan seemed to be to wear out their enemy. Daily the odds against the French grew; for shiploads of redcoats would move up and down with the strong tide and keep Bougainville's wretched, half-starved men tramping and scrambling along the rough ground of the heights in order to follow and forestall this puzzling and persistent enemy.

On the 10th a French officer near the Foulon, one of the posts on the heights between Quebec and Cap Rouge, saw, through his telescope, that six British officers on the south shore were carefully surveying the heights all about him. When he reported this at once, Montcalm tried again to reinforce this point. He also tried to send a good officer to command the Foulon post. The officer stationed there was Vergor, one of the Bigot gang and a great friend of Vaudreuil's. Vergor had disgraced himself by giving up Fort Beausejour in Acadia without a fight. He was now disgracing himself again by allowing fifty of the hundred men at the post to go and work at their farms in the valley of the St Charles, provided that they put in an equal amount of work on his own farm there. It was a bad feature of the case that his utter worthlessness was as well known to Wolfe as it was to Montcalm.

On the 11th and 12th the movements of the fleet became more puzzling than before. They still seemed, however, to point to a landing somewhere along those much threatened thirteen miles between Cap Rouge and Pointe aux Trembles, but, more especially, at Pointe aux Trembles itself. By this time Bougainville's 2,000 men were fairly worn out with constant marching to and fro; and on the evening of the 12th they were for the most part too tired to cook their suppers. Bougainville kept the bulk of them for the night near St Augustin, five miles below Pointe aux Trembles and eight miles above Cap Rouge, so that he could go to either end of his line when he made his inspection in the morning. He knew that at sunset some British vessels were still off Pointe aux Trembles. He knew also that most of the British vessels had gone down for the night to St Nicholas, on the south shore, only four miles nearer Quebec than he was at St Augustin. Bougainville and everybody else on both sides—except Wolfe and Montcalm themselves—thought the real attack was going to be made close to Pointe aux Trembles, for news had leaked out that this was the plan formed by the British brigadiers with Wolfe's own approval.

Down the river, below Quebec, in his six miles of entrenchments at Beauport, Montcalm was getting more and more uneasy on the fatal 12th. Where was Wolfe's army? The bulk of it, two brigades, was said to be at St Nicholas, thirteen miles above Quebec, facing the same thirteen miles that Bougainville's worn-out men had been so long defending. But where was Wolfe's third brigade? Saunders remained opposite Beauport, as usual. His boats seemed very busy laying buoys, as if to mark out good landing-places for another attack. He had redcoats with him, too. Which were they? Marines? Soldiers? Nobody could see. There were more redcoats at the island of Orleans, more at the Point of Levy, more still near the Levis batteries. Were these all soldiers or were some of them marines? Why was Saunders beginning to bombard the entrenchments at Beauport and to send boats along the shore there after dark? Was this a feint or not? Why were the Levis batteries thundering so furiously against Quebec? Was it to cover Wolfe's crowded boats coming down to join Saunders at Beauport?

Montcalm was up all night, keeping his men ready for anything. That night Bougainville reported much the same news as for several days past. He expected to see Holmes and Wolfe back at Pointe aux Trembles in the morning. If occasion arose, he was, however, ready to march down to Cap Rouge as fast as his tired-out men could go. His thirteen miles were being well watched.

What, however, about the nine miles of shore under his guard between Cap Rouge and Quebec? About them Vaudreuil was as stubborn as ever. They were a line of high cliffs, seemingly impregnable, and Vergor who defended them was his friend. Surely this was enough! But Montcalm saw what a chance the position offered to a man of such daring skill as Wolfe. Again he tried to have Vergor recalled, but in vain. Then, in the afternoon of the 12th, he took the bold but the only safe course of ordering the Guienne battalion, four hundred strong, to go up at once and camp for the night at the top of the Foulon, near Vergor. The men were all ready to march off when Vaudreuil found out what they were going to do. It was no order of his! It would belittle him to let Montcalm take his place! And, anyhow, it was all nonsense! Raising his voice so that the staff could hear him, he then said: 'The English haven't wings! Let La Guienne stay where it is! I'll see about that Foulon myself tomorrow morning!'

'Tomorrow morning' began early, long before Vergor and Vaudreuil were out of bed. Of the two Vergor was up first; up first, and with a shock, to find redcoats running at his tent with fixed bayonets. He was off, like a flash, in his nightshirt, and Wolfe had taken his post. He ought to have been on the alert for friends as well as foes that early morning, because all the French posts had been warned to look out for a provision convoy which was expected down the north shore and in at the Foulon itself. But Vergor was asleep instead, and half his men were away at his farm. So Vaudreuil lost his chance to 'see about that Foulon himself' on that 'tomorrow morning.'

Saunders had been threatening the entrenchments at Beauport all night, and before daylight the Levis batteries had redoubled their fire against Quebec. But about five o'clock Montcalm's quick ear caught the sound of a new cannonade above Quebec. It came from the Foulon, which was only two miles and a half from the St Charles bridge of boats, though the tableland of the Plains of Abraham rose between, three hundred feet high. Montcalm's first thought was for the provision convoy, so badly needed in his half-starved camp. He knew it was expected down at the Foulon 'this very night, and that the adjacent Samos battery was to try to protect it from the British men-of-war as it ran in. But he did not know that it had been stopped by a British frigate above Pointe aux Trembles, and that Wolfe's boats were taking its place and fooling the French sentries, who had been ordered to pass it quietly.

Yet he knew Wolfe; he knew Vergor; and now the sound of the cannonade alarmed him. Setting spurs to his horse, he galloped down from Beauport to the bridge of boats, giving orders as he went to turn out every man at once.

At the bridge he found Vaudreuil writing a letter to Bougainville. If Vaudreuil had written nothing else in his life, this single letter would

Comte de Bougainville

be enough to condemn him forever at the bar of history. With the British on the Plains of Abraham and the fate of half a continent trembling in the scale, he prattled away on his official foolscap as if Wolfe was at the head of only a few naughty boys whom a squad of police could easily arrest. '*I have set the army in motion. I have sent the Marquis of Montcalm with one hundred Canadians as a reinforcement.*'

Montcalm took up with him a good many more than the 'one hundred Canadians' Vaudreuil ordered him to take, and he sent to Bougainville a message very different from the one Vaudreuil had written. What hero was ever more sorely tried? When he caught sight of the redcoats marching towards Quebec, in full view of the place where Vaudreuil was writing that idiotic letter, he exclaimed, as he well might:'Ah! there they are, where they have no right to be!' Then, turning to the officers with him, he added: 'Gentlemen, this is a serious affair. Let everyone take post at once!'

The camp was already under arms. Montcalm ordered up all the French and Canadian regulars and all the militia, except 2,000. Vaudreuil at once ordered a battalion of regulars and all the militia, except 2,000, to stay where they were. Montcalm asked for the whole of the twenty-five field guns in Quebec. Vaudreuil gave him three.

Wolfe's 5,000 redcoats were already on the Plains when Montcalm galloped up to the crest of ground from which he could see them, only six hundred yards away. The line was very thin, only two-deep, and its right did not seem to have come up yet. Some sailors were dragging up a gun, not far from the Foulon. Perhaps Wolfe's landing was not quite completed?

Meanwhile half the 5,000 that Montcalm was able to get into action was beginning to fire at the redcoats from under cover and at some distance. This half was militia and Indians, 2,000 of the first and 500 of the second. The flat and open battlefield that Wolfe had in his front was almost empty. It was there that Montcalm would have to fight with his other 2,500, in eight small battalions of regulars—five French and three Canadian.

These regulars wasted no time, once they were clear of Vaudreuil, who still thought some of them should stay down at Montmorency. They crossed the bridge of boats and the valley of the St Charles, mounted the Heights of Abraham, and formed up about as far on the inner side of the crest of ground as Wolfe's men were on the outer side. Montcalm called his brigadiers, colonels, and staff together, to find out if anyone could explain the movements of the British. No one knew anything certain. But most of them thought that the enemy's line was not yet complete, and that, for this reason, as well as because the sailors were beginning to land entrenching tools and artillery, it would be better to attack at once.

Montcalm agreed. In fact, he had no choice. He was now completely cut off from the St Lawrence above Quebec. His army could not be fed by land for another week. Most important of all, by prompt action he might get in a blow before Wolfe was quite ready. There was nothing to wait for. Bougainville must have started down the river bank, as hard as his tired-out men could march. To wait for French reinforcements meant to wait for British ones too, and the British would gain more by reinforcements than the French. The fleet was closing in. Boats crowded with marines and sailors were rowing to the Foulon, with tools and guns for a siege. Already a naval brigade was on the beach.

Montcalm gave the signal, the eight battalions stepped off, reached the crest of the hill, and came in sight of their opponents. Wolfe's front was of six battalions two-deep, about equal in numbers to Montcalm's eight battalions six-deep. The redcoats marched forward a hundred paces and halted. The two fronts were now a quarter of a mile apart. Wolfe's front represented the half of his army. Some of the other half were curved back to protect the flanks against the other half of Montcalm's; and some were in reserve, ready for Bougainville.

Montcalm rode along his little line for the last time. There stood the heroes of his four great victories—Oswego, Fort William Henry, Ticonderoga, Montmorency. He knew that at least half of them would follow wherever he led. The three Canadian battalions on his right and left might not close with an enemy who had bayonets and knew how to use them, when they themselves had none. The Languedoc battalion of Frenchmen was also a little shaky, because it had been obliged to take most of the bad recruits sent out to replace the tried soldiers captured by the British fleet in 1755. But the remainder were true as steel.

'Don't you want a little rest before you begin?' asked Montcalm, as he passed the veteran Royal Roussillon.

'No, no; we're never tired before a battle!' the men shouted back. And so he rode along, stopping to say a word to each battalion on the way. He had put on his full uniform that morning, thinking a battle might be fought. He wore the green, gold-embroidered coat he had worn at court when he presented his son to the king and took leave of

France for ever. It was open in front, showing his polished cuirass. The Grand Cross of St Louis glittered on his breast, over as brave a heart as any of the Montcalms had shown during centuries in the presence of the foe. From head to foot he looked the hero that he was; and he sat his jet-black charger as if the horse and man were one.

He reined up beside the Languedoc battalion, hoping to steady it by leading it in person. As he did so he saw that the Canadians and Indians were pressing Wolfe's flanks more closely from under cover and that there was some confusion in the thin red line itself, where its skirmishers, having been called in, were trying to find their places in too much of a hurry. This was his only chance. Up went his sword, and the advance began, the eight six-deep battalions stepping off together at the slow march, with shouldered arms. 'Long live the King and Montcalm!' they shouted, as they had shouted at Ticonderoga; and the ensigns waved the *fleurs-de-lis* aloft.

Half the distance was covered in good formation. But when the three battalions of Canadian regulars came within musket-shot they suddenly began to fire without orders, and then dropped down flat to reload. This threw out the line; and there was more wavering when the French saw that the Canadians, far from regaining their places, were running off to the flanks to join the militia and Indians under cover. Montcalm was now left with only his five French battalions— five short, thick lines, four white and one blue, against Wolfe's long, six-jointed, thin red line. He halted a moment, to steady the men, and advanced again in the way that regulars at that time fought each other on flat and open battlefields: a short march of fifty paces or so, in slow time, a halt to fire, another advance and another halt to fire, until the foes came to close quarters, when a bayonet charge gave the victory to whichever side had kept its formation the better.

A single British gun was firing grape-shot straight into the French left and cutting down a great many men. But the thin red line itself was silent; silent as the grave and steadfast as a wall. Presently the substitutes in the Languedoc battalion could not endure the strain any longer. They fired without orders and could not be stopped. At the same time Montcalm saw that his five little bodies of men were drifting apart. When the Canadian regulars had moved off, they had left the French flanks quite open. In consequence, the French battalions nearest the flanks kept edging outwards, the ones on the right towards their own right and the ones on the left towards their own left, to prevent themselves from being overlapped by the long red line of fire and steel when the two fronts closed. But this drift outwards, while not enough to reach Wolfe's flanks, was quite enough to make a fatal gap in Montcalm's centre. Thus the British, at the final moment, took the French on both the outer and both the inner flanks as well as straight in front.

The separating distance was growing less and less. A hundred paces now! Would that grim line of redcoats never fire? Seventy-five!!—Fifty!!—Forty!!!—the glint of a sword-blade on the British right!—the word of command to their grenadiers!—'Ready!—Present!—Fire!!!' Like six single shots from as many cannon the British volleys crashed forth, from right to left, battalion by battalion, all down that thin red line.

The stricken front rank of the French fell before these double-shotted volleys almost to a man. When the smoke cleared off the British had come nearer still. They had closed up twenty paces to their front, reloading as they came. And now, taking the six-deep French in front and flanks, they fired as fast as they could, but steadily and under perfect control. The French, on the other hand, were firing wildly, and simply crumbling away before that well-aimed storm of lead. The four white lines melted into shapeless masses. They rocked and reeled like sinking vessels. In a vain, last effort to lead them on, their officers faced death and found it. All three brigadiers and two of the colonels went down. Montcalm was the only one of four French generals still on horseback; and he was wounded while trying to keep the Languedoc men in action.

Suddenly, on the right, the Sarre and Languedoc battalions turned and ran. A moment more, and Bearn and Guienne, in the centre, had followed them. The wounded Montcalm rode alone among the mad rush of panic-stricken fugitives. But over towards the St Lawrence cliffs he saw the blue line of the Royal Roussillon still fighting desperately against the overlapping redcoats. He galloped up to them. But, even as he arrived, the whole mass swayed, turned, and broke in wild confusion. Only three officers remained. Half the battalion was killed or wounded. Nothing could stay its flight.

On the top of the crest of ground, where he had formed his line of attack only a few minutes before, Montcalm was trying to rally some men to keep back the pursuing British when he was hit again, and this time he received a mortal wound. He reeled in the saddle, and would have fallen had not two faithful grenadiers sprung to his side and held him up. His splendid black charger seemed to know what was the matter with his master, and walked on gently at a foot's pace down the Grande Allee and into Quebec by the St Louis Gate. Pursuers and pursued were now racing for the valley of the St Charles, and Quebec itself was, for the moment, safe.

Never was there a greater rout than on the Plains of Abraham at ten o'clock that morning. The French and Canadians ran for the bridge of boats, their only safety. But they came very close to being cut off both in front and rear. Vaudreuil had poked his nose out of one of the gates of Quebec when the flight began. He then galloped down to the bridge, telling the Canadians on the Cote d'Abraham, which was the road from the Plains to the St Charles, to make a stand there. Having got safely over the bridge himself, he was actually having it cut adrift, when some officers rushed up and stopped this crowning act of shame. This saved the fugitives in front of the broken army.

Meanwhile the flying troops were being saved in the rear by the Canadians at the Cote d'Abraham under a French officer called Dumas. These Canadians had not done much in the battle, for various reasons: one was that the fighting was in the open, a mode of warfare in which they had not been trained; the British, moreover, used bayonets, of which the Canadians themselves had none. But in the bush along the crest of the cliffs overlooking the valley they fought splendidly. After holding back the pursuit for twenty minutes, and losing a quarter of their numbers, they gave way. Then a few of them made a second stand at a mill and bakery in the valley itself, and were killed or wounded to a man.

Montcalm heard the outburst of firing at the Cote d'Abraham. But he knew that all was over now, that Canada was lost, and with it all he had fought for so nobly, so wisely, and so well. As he rode through St Louis Gate, with the two grenadiers holding him up in his saddle, a terrified woman shrieked out: 'Oh! look at the *marquis*, he's killed, he's killed!'

'It is nothing at all, my kind friend,' answered Montcalm, trying to sit up straight, 'you must not be so much alarmed!' Five minutes later the doctor told him he had only a few hours to live. 'So much the better,' he replied; 'I shall not see the surrender of Quebec.'

On hearing that he had such a short time before him his first thought was to leave no possible duty undone. He told the commandant of Quebec that he had no advice to give about the surrender. He told Vaudreuil's messenger that there were only three courses for the army to follow: to fight again, surrender, or retreat towards Montreal;

and that he would advise a retreat. He dictated a letter to the British commander. It was written by his devoted secretary, Marcel, and delivered to Wolfe's successor, Townshend:

> Sir, being obliged to surrender Quebec to your arms I have the honour to recommend our sick and wounded to Your Excellency's kindness, and to ask you to carry out the exchange of prisoners, as agreed upon between His Most Christian Majesty and His Britannic Majesty. I beg Your Excellency to rest assured of the high esteem and great respect with which I have the honour to be your most humble and obedient servant,
>
> Montcalm.

And then, his public duty over, he sent a message to each member of his family at Candiac, including 'poor Mirete,' for not a word had come from France since the British fleet had sealed up the St Lawrence, and he did not yet know which of his daughters had died.

Having remembered his family he gave the rest of his thoughts to his God and to that other world he was so soon to enter. All night long his lips were seen to move in prayer. And, just as the dreary dawn was breaking; he breathed his last.

War is the grave of the Montcalms.